FARM POLICY: 13 ESSAYS

FARM POLICY: 13 ESSAYS

HAROLD F. BREIMYER

HD
1759
.B74

Iowa State University Press
Ames Iowa

HAROLD F. BREIMYER, Perry Foundation Professor of Agricultural Economics and Extension Economist at the University of Missouri-Columbia, holds a joint appointment in teaching, research, and extension. His field is marketing and public policy. Educated at Ohio State University, University of California, and American University, in 1936 he became an economist with the United States Department of Agriculture. After holding various government positions he joined the University of Missouri in 1966. He was President of the American Agricultural Economics Association in 1969, and in 1973 was named a Fellow of that organization. He is the author of *Economics of the Product Markets of Agriculture* (1976).

© 1977 The Iowa State University Press
Ames, Iowa 50010. All rights reserved

Composed and printed by
The Iowa State University Press

First edition, 1977

Library of Congress Cataloging in Publication Data
Breimyer, Harold F
    Farm policy.
    Includes bibliographical references and index.
    CONTENTS: Biological man and social organization.—Agrarian agriculture.—The (partial) industrialization of agriculture.—[etc.]
    1. Agriculture and state—United States—Addresses, essays, lectures. 2. Agriculture—Economic aspects—United States—Addresses, essays, lectures. I. Title.
HD1759.B74   338.1'873   77-9594
ISBN 0-8138-0645-3

THE 13 ESSAYS

PREFACE

A century and a half ago the French chronicler of America Alexis de Tocqueville noted a paradox in rural America between the drive for individual freedom and the attraction of combining in order to get the benefits of power. In 1976 Don Hadwiger developed the idea of paradox at some length. He said, poetically, that paradox is the farmer's most important product. The thirteen essays presented here touch on the Tocqueville paradox but present many others too. They begin by noting distinctions between material content and social organization in agriculture. They acknowledge differences between crop and animal agriculture. Quickly thereafter they contrast the ancient agrarian root of farming and the industrial aspects that are now superimposed on it, a pairing that serves almost as a theme for this small volume.

The thirteen pieces are indeed essays, discursive and neither closely interconnected nor free of overlap. They are intended to prick, stimulate, stir imaginations, and above all to teach. Although opinions are not absent the essays present no prescription for policy. They are not a tract of advocacy.

In large measure this book traces from my professional writings as a staff member at the University of Missouri, especially those in Extension Public Affairs. Two extension letters are reproduced in full as an appendix.

Gratitude is due my colleagues, V. James Rhodes and Robert J. Bevins, and Lauren Soth for their critical review of earlier drafts, and Ms. Judy Hamilton for converting rough copy to neat typography.

If dedication *en bloc* be permissible, it is to those many persons, most of them unidentified, who do me the courtesy of reading my monthly extension letters as well as other publications.

HAROLD F. BREIMYER

FARM POLICY: 13 ESSAYS

The human brain, so fragile, so perishable, so full of inexhaustible dreams and hungers, burns by the power of the leaf.
—LOREN EISELEY

1 BIOLOGICAL MAN AND SOCIAL ORGANIZATION

Policy for agriculture has two roots. One is biological, the other anthropological. The former embraces living organisms in general and the resources and processes for their support. The latter is confined to one such organism, the human being.

So familiar as to pall is the fact that all human existence rests on the magic that chlorophyll performs as it converts the sun's rays into the carbohydrates of plant tissue. The enzymes of the alimentary system complete the support sequence as they transform the energy ingested (directly or via animal products) to empower motor or cerebral activity.

From primitive foraging to modern scientific farming, agriculture is the domain for the processes of human sustenance. Physically those processes involve the biology of plants and animals and the soil as supporting culture. Together these form the agrarian portion of agriculture, which is described in Chapter 2.

But agriculture is more than agrarianism. The provisioning of human beings is a managed process. It is not fortuitous. Probably it never has been. Primitive people may have been random harvesters, but they were hardly isolated or careless ones. They surely were quick to extend skills learned in collecting nuts and trapping animals to rational and purposeful activity. Moreover, they put them in social context. In all likelihood a rudimentary social arrangement was formed early in collecting and preparing food. Ever since, cooperative endeavor has marked most of human beings' efforts to feed themselves.

Thus we arrive at human direction, the role of brain power.

This becomes the first of the paradoxes promised in the foreword to these essays. Or perhaps it is just a case of closely cycled circularity. Captured and transformed energy fuels the human brain which in turn organizes the capturing and transforming process. Hence the relevance of the opening quotation from the famed scientist Loren Eiseley.

The managing of today's agriculture lifts it beyond agrarianism. In language often used it is being industrialized. This is an American version of the German term rationalization. It means only that more controlled order is being brought to agriculture.

Many of the issues in agricultural policy revolve around the means for arriving at that order. Because the industrialization part of policy is so prominent it is reviewed at length in Chapter 3. The built-in conflict between the agrarian and the industrial features of modern agriculture is also described there. That conflict goes far to explain why farm policy is so inconsistent, discordant, hard to arrive at.

The means for organizing and managing agriculture—the essence of policy—leads to a wide variety of individual policy issues. What is to be the managerial unit and how are units to be interconnected? What is the place of group organization? What is the role of government?

Management in agriculture has an intergenerational dimension. This imposes stern tests. It requires that a moral choice be made between generations—ours, and those of the future. To protect the future requires, unavoidably, some denial of the present. How far ahead do we look? Do we, like Banquo's ghost, see an endless string of generations? Or is our planning present-generation egocentric?

FARMING AND AGRICULTURE

The words "farming" and "agriculture" are lodged deep in the American vocabulary. Literary roots of the words suggest that significant distinctions can be made. Some differences are of class or status. By some accounts farming is low caste and agriculture high. Other distinctions bear on how inclusive each term is.

The Snobbery Coefficient

The question as to how high farming and the people who farm rank on the social and political scale is at once ancient and modern. James Horsfall suggests that farming has long been regarded as a dirty word. The verb to farm has obscure English-French roots. It apparently traces to the Old French *fermer,* to fix or make a contract, which in turn derives from the Latin *firmare,* to make firm. Horsfall translates this into the role of the farmer as a renter: "a farmer in the Old French was a share cropper, a peasant, a serf." It's all low brow.

Agriculture is different. The word clearly comes from the Latin, *ager,* the field, and *cultura,* cultivation. Cultivation, says Horsfall, is high brow and even implies excellence of taste (1).

If U.S. farmers were to take their language seriously they doubtless would opt for esteemed agriculture over scorned farming. On the other

hand, most farmers are indifferent to language and hold their heads
high irrespective of the lexicon.

The Fields and the Flocks

Much more significant is how inclusive each term, farming and agriculture, is. Agriculture is literally cultivation of the field. What about
animal culture? Historically, did domestication of animals precede or
follow cultivation of land? Probably the latter but whatever the order,
the relation of animal to land culture presents an enigma to this day.
Even our language betrays the discord. Land is "tilled" and crops
"planted," mechanical words, but care of animals comes under the
term "husbandry," which connotes human involvement.

Perhaps, as the lyricist put it, the plowman and the cowman should
be friends. They have not often been so. More frequently they have
been rivals if not antagonists.

The conflict is sharpest where livestock are grazed. There animal
and crop culture are parallel and competitive. They compete for status.
They also compete for land because even nomads prefer level plain to
rocky hillside. Historic rivalry is recounted in the Bible as early as the
fourth chapter of Genesis, where the first recorded homicide is attributed
to it. In the frontier U.S. West bloody nightriding forays between
ranchers and "farmers" (cultivators) helped the region earn the adjective
"Wild."

Modern practice is to pamper livestock and poultry by feeding
them ground grain in sheltered surroundings. Thereby crop and animal
culture become separate enterprises, irrespective of whether they are
managed together.

Where crop and animal enterprises are combined on the same farm
they are essentially complementary, although they may compete for labor
at some seasons. Where specialization disjoins the two, competitiveness
and even discord again come into view. Language follows suit. Producing crops and livestock on the same (family) farm is still called "farming" or "agriculture." But are large-scale units in cattle feeding or poultry that resemble manufacturing called agriculture?

Where federal farm policy is involved cattle-feeding and poultry
units are virtually excluded. When the U.S. Congress deliberates over
policy, it concentrates on crops. It gives passing attention to dairying
and cattle ranching, and virtually disregards large-scale cattle feeding,
broilers, and eggs.

On the other hand, the U.S. Department of Agriculture still counts
Cargill's and Allied Mills's broiler profits in farm income, though with
apologetic tongue in cheek. When those two firms and a number of
others saw fit to invoke the protection of the Capper-Volstead law for
some of their joint projects on grounds that they are farmers, the U.S.
Department of Justice said "Nay." The District Court reversed Justice,

but the Appeals Court reversed the District Court's ruling. As of mid-1977, Cargill and Allied are not chicken farmers protected by Capper-Volstead.

So what is agriculture? The term is in limbo. However, a separation seems to be underway as commercial livestock and poultry operations are increasingly excluded.

Because popular usage draws no sharp definitional lines none will be followed in these essays. But one rule of thumb may help. The next chapter explains that farming (or agriculture) is distinguished by the resource of the land. Accordingly, whatever is tied reasonably tightly to the land can be included. Livestock enterprises that stay closely connected are still a part of farming, or of agriculture. Egg cities and giant feedlots for cattle hardly qualify.

A MORAL ATTRIBUTION

Human beings seem ever disposed to attach moral precepts to their arrangements for making a living. They have surely done so regarding agriculture. Agriculture, always acknowledged as fundamental to existence, has also been credited with moral properties—the capacity to engender in human beings an elevated behavior. This philosophy is "agricultural fundamentalism" (2).

Without a hint of disbelief we can wonder at the origin for such attribution. Is it rooted deeply in the essentialness of food and fiber? Food and clothing are indeed essential but so are some other things, even minimum social contact. Another possible explanation is our knowledge that land is unique in character and finite in quantity. Crops and livestock cannot be produced without it. Does this logic account for the primacy assigned to agriculture?

One thesis is that the processes of nature teach personal discipline. Surely nature imposes imperious demands and levies penalties for violating her orders. It is entirely plausible that even in today's sophisticated urban society we retain rules of moral conduct that have agrarian origin.

The irony in all this is that cultivation of land lost its primary character when outside materials were introduced. These may have begun as the simplest hand tools. Today they embrace an elaborate display of machines, fuels, chemicals, and dozens of lesser materials. These in turn have their own origin, principally in mines and oil and gas wells. So is agriculture primary?

ORGANIZATIONAL LESSONS, IF ANY

If farm policy is a question of the organization and management of agriculture, it is fair to ask whether agriculture also has organizational lessons to teach.

To philosophize, an old question asks to what extent physical surroundings influence human social organization. Karl Marx was noted for emphasizing scientific materialism, the doctrine that material circumstances shape the social system. The idea is persuasive. In agriculture, do the sun and soil determine our food-supplying system? Or do our ideologies do so? Perhaps the two interact.

We observed in opening lines that getting food has always involved working together. The first efforts may have yielded rudimentary principles for social organization. From social lessons learned in collective action to supply food, prophets and teachers drew general principles about how human beings interact responsibly.

Ancient peoples organized themselves around internally self-sufficient units of modest size. They began with extended families or tribes. They had internal government. In Greek and Roman times estates emerged. Roman writers on agriculture delved into principles of their management. Works of Cato and Varro, which once were assigned reading to budding agricultural economists, were treatises on management. Did management of estates then provide both the operating nucleus and the instructional wisdom for forming larger social entities—the modern corporation, the city-state, the nation?

In the vast rural expanse of the Soviet Union the collective farm is not only a unit for producing wheat and milk but also the means for providing social services and town government.

In the United States the academic discipline of agricultural economics has always combined farm management and farm policy. It still does so. Whether by drift or design, management of farm enterprises and management of people who manage enterprises are combined in a single area of scientific inquiry.

To a considerable extent agriculture and the rural community together form a distinctive organizational entity, even in cosmopolitan United States. We ask again, now as anciently, do agriculture and its community have a social-organizational lesson to teach? Can it be instructive to the rest of our nation?

Or is our traditional kind of agriculture itself now an anachronism, bereft of example-value and ticketed for oblivion?

THE SCOPE OF INQUIRY

It's a long stretch from the biology of capturing the sun's rays for human nutrition to the principles of organizing managerial units in agriculture, and from there to agriculture's model-setting and teaching role to society. An inquiry into farm policy today spans such a gamut. Of such is farm policy made. Essays that follow will range that far, though without pretense of completeness.

NOTES

1. James G. Horsfall, "Agricultural Strategy in the Tragedy of the Commons," *Agricultural Science Review,* U.S. Dept. of Agr., first quarter 1972, p. 19.
2. See the second essay in the appendix, and the reference given there to a famous article by Joseph Davis.

It is agriculture which furnishes the material of industry and commerce and which pays both; but these two branches give back their gain to agriculture, which renews the wealth.
—Francois Quesnay (French Physiocrat)

2 AGRARIAN AGRICULTURE

On the winter banquet circuit in farming communities no theme has been more popular, more certain to draw audience applause, than that agriculture has been emancipated from its dreary agrarian past. Agriculture is now, so the orators say, a modern high-technology undertaking.

"Farming is no longer a way of life but a business" is offered as the ultimate accolade. It is voiced in boring repetitiveness despite the fact that farming has long been both, as are school teaching, feed selling, politicking, and gunrunning for the Mafia. People in every occupation blend the cultural and money-grubbing halves of their lives. Farming is no different.

What agriculture of our era does is combine a technology of non-farm origin with the basic resource of land. It is an addition and not a displacement. Agriculture has not been detached from its agrarian base of the land. On the contrary it holds tenaciously to that ancient connection. The land base is still essential. But to it are added all the materials and techniques that are the gift of science and industry.

The two do not fit well. Agrarian traits, retained as persistently as the white-face gene in Hereford crossbreeding, stand in constant conflict with the systematic order and centralized control that are the hallmark of industrial processes.

Farmers, their families, and their organizational system are caught in the disharmony. The conflict reaches even to the survivability of the traditional kind of farm and farmer. The agrarian side of farming is defensive of the independent proprietary farm unit. The industrial side would doom it. When two trends tug in opposite directions, what is to be the outcome?

Contrasting agrarian and industrial influences give us a nexus for examining a variety of issues in agricultural policy, here and in later chapters.

THE UNIQUENESS OF LAND

Except for a trivial amount of hydroponics and feeding a few synthetic nutrients to livestock, all agriculture is unalterably based on land. Not all the magic of chemistry can replace fertile soil as an indispensable resource for producing food and natural fiber.

Land has won humanity's testimony to its powers of succor. Poeticized as Earth, its virtues have been sung by troubador, proclaimed by priest, and modestly bowed to by grateful peasant. To the Jew and Christian "The Earth is the Lord's." The nonchurched Russian hallows his Mother Earth.

Land enters deeply into secular institutions too, and not always so benignly. In all agrarian societies the rules governing access to land and division of its bounty go far to account for both the family structure and prevailing economic system.

Land has been searched for, by restless nomads and aggressive explorers.

Land has been fought over, a thousand thousand times.

Land has been appropriated by the strong to control and exploit the weak.

Land has been a promise of opportunity but also, far too often, a seat of bondage.

Land has made some people rich. Its unavailability has impoverished more.

Five Characteristics

In less poetic and more analytic language, land has five characteristics that from the standpoint of agricultural policy overshadow all others.

1. Land is an inherited resource. Human effort can improve it but not create it. The devout may call it God-Given. The scientist may explain that water, weather, and the accumulated humus of decayed plants interact to convert it from rock. In any case, it is not man-made.

Each generation must subsist on the land delivered to it from its forebears.

2. The counterpart is that land can be an everlasting resource. With care it can be kept productive indefinitely. Hence the religious assurance that God has provided for his children, from generation unto generation.

But it can be destroyed. The admonition follows for good stewardship.

3. Land is virtually worthless of itself, and is made productive only through human labor. Admittedly, natural cover will yield some foodstuffs, but even they must be harvested.

4. Land is not homogeneous. Far from it, land is highly variable in its responsiveness to the labor brought to bear upon it and also to industrial materials such as chemical fertilizer applied to it.

5. Significantly, though, the responsiveness to labor or industrial material takes on a characteristic pattern. It is the familiar pattern of increasing and decreasing marginal physical returns. The first unit of labor applied brings little produce from land; the second adds more, and so on until a maximum marginal return is obtained. Then the marginal return starts downward. It eventually goes down fast and can finally become negative.

Land as a Medium

In a practical sense land is only a medium, a carrier vehicle. In a process powered by sunlight, water carrying minerals in solution combines with carbon dioxide and nitrogen from the air to produce carbohydrates useful to human beings. Human effort directs and protects the process, to the aim of a bountiful yield.

In another sense, in the language of an industrial era land is the ultimate capital good. It preexisted its tenants of any age and will survive them.

Land is truly a unique resource.

THE BIOLOGY OF FARMING

If land is a unique resource required for the biology that sustains all life including human life, farming of that land has distinctive attributes.

At least five characteristics of farming may be named, adding to the five features of land.

1. Farming involves a great number of individual processes. It truly requires versatile expertise. Not even the assembly of so complex a machine as a Ford automobile, done in a long conveyor-belt assembly line, entails as many and as diverse skills as does cropping or animal-raising in agriculture. From the chemistry of soils to the nursing of a sick cow to coaxing a balky tractor motor to figuring the annual income tax, an array of abilities is called for.

2. In even sharper contrast with assembling a Ford car is the sequential order that nature and animal biology jointly impose on agriculture. The Ford can be assembled in a morning as each of a hundred workers "does his thing." Planting of a crop cannot be done simultaneously with harvesting, nor breeding of cattle with their slaughter.

The late John Brewster, among others, saw nonsimultaneity as the principal reason agriculture cannot adopt the techniques of manufacturing widely.

3. The cropping and grazing portion of agriculture is geographically extensive. As a worldwide average, more than half an acre of cultivated land is required to support each human being. Whether because

of limited sunlight, water, or minerals, or because more efficient germ plasm of plants remains to be developed—whatever the reason, cropping of land is an extensive enterprise.

4. Caring for crops and livestock as biological organisms requires a diligence that has no counterpart in industrial manufacturing. Even though the assembly of a Ford involves disciplined, responsible performance, the assembly line can be shut down and the building padlocked. But orchards must be sprayed in season, corn planted in brief interludes between rains, and cows milked morning and night.

"Who will sit up with the corporate sow?" was the image-inducing title that the Center for Rural Affairs chose for its report on corporate hog production. Perhaps a corporate employee will do so; but the question is properly asked.

5. As taken from the land most farm products are bulky and perishable. Eggs and oil-bearing fruits and nuts may be nutritionally the most concentrated raw products of agriculture. Feedstuffs are the most bulky. Fresh fruits and milk are perhaps the most perishable.

LAND, FARMING, AND SOCIAL INSTITUTIONS
The chemistry of soil and water, the imperious chronology of the seasons, and the fragile biology of plant and animal life make up a powerful force shaping human institutions for wringing subsistence from land.

Gaining Access to Land
The attributes of land help to explain why from time immemorial it has been the object of so much contest. As land is not a product of man's making, having no human creator, the stage is set for dispute over how to determine access to it. Probably access has been gained more often by force than by any other means.

If access is to be arranged peacefully, questions arise as to what the terms are to be. One philosophy is that what man has not made he dare not self-appropriate. Or, if he be permitted to do so—that is, if private ownership of land be allowed—custom and law will dictate certain conditions. Towering over all other conditions is that land be used for the common good. Built into social mores and the lore of farmers is the plea that land be kept productive. Countless ceremonies—farmers' own rituals, blue ribbons at a fair, tributes from Rotary Club, press, and political platform—shower blessings on those who comply.

In farmers' own gratification system the sense of performing a life-sustaining service is not minor.

Institutions for private ownership of land, where they prevail, are of the nature of a social concession with revocable strings attached. In most Western systems land is conveyed by title. This means entitlement, the opportunity to enjoy certain privileges in exchange for assuming certain obligations. Landholding institutions are not of the same character as buying a shirt, a steak, or a snowmobile.

Private ownership without need for much surveillance comes easiest in new territories where land is plentiful and cheap. As populations crowd upon land, the contingency of public concern, never relinquished, begins to show up. It appears in calls for watershed protection, preserving wilderness, keeping land in recreation or forest, or zoning nonfarm uses. Landholders' understandable protest can grow to turmoil if the issues are not resolved amicably.

Social Institutions for Farming
Through most of history human beings have wrung their subsistence from soil and have distributed it among themselves by organizing into collective units approaching self-sufficiency.

This seems strange to American minds. In the United States today we think of the independent proprietary ("family") farm as the prototype arrangement. It has been for us. It has not been for others. It has been rare historically. Private small-farm landholding flourished briefly in early Greece and Rome. It made other spot appearances. It seldom survived for long.

By analogy it cannot be expected to last much longer in the United States and other Western nations. Its prospect for doing so, and the public question whether to prolong its tenure, are policy issues of first importance today.

Ancient Integration
During ancient and middle ages, far more common than the yeoman farmer were mutual support units that probably began with the nomadic tribe. Later there came the Greek or Roman estate, as was noted in Chapter 1. This was followed by the medieval manor, the Spanish hacienda, the old-English grazing commons, and the plantation of our antebellum South.

Closest approximation in our day to old composite farming units is the kibbutz of Israel or, perhaps even more so, the collective farm of the Soviet Union. Although the Soviet kolkholz (collective) bears some of the marks of an industrial agriculture, in other respects it is a throwback to the Roman estate.

No happenstance, the self-sufficient collective of history was a logical outcome of its circumstances. When geography was a barrier to communication yet diverse skills and division of labor were necessary, a multifamily organizational unit was sensible. It was the unit best able to survive.

Moreover, clustering in villages gave physical protection in those centuries before a rural gendarmerie, predecessor of our sheriffs and state highway patrols, provided protection against brigands. It is not inconceivable that the growing frequency of rural crime in our day will send farm families scurrying once more to the protection of a village.

Internal Government of Agrarian Units. Collective units for self-suffi-ciency always require internal government. Methods of providing it have varied widely. The most considerate or liberal have relied on custom or convention. The most authoritarian have centered power in a head or chief, who can be despotic.

Internal government of any organization invariably sways toward one or the other of these extremes, says Professor John Hicks, noted English economist. In his language the first rests on a "corpus of tradi-tion," but the second presents an autocratic "power center" (1).

However brought about, the governmental system for integrated agrarian units ruled over internal operations. It controlled assignment of duties and distribution of rewards.

To say that these various versions of internal government became prototype for governmental systems for larger communities, city-states, and nations is not to claim too much. On the other hand, to credit them with being generally enlightened would be erroneous. A few were, but many were not. The old agrarian tradition was not democratic. (See Appendix II.)

Independent Unit Agriculture
Not the agrarian units of the old world but the farms of the new United States, with an accompanying market system, are the most original social contribution agriculture has made. Aided by access to unlimited land, the old system of extended-family units was replaced by one of inde-pendent units that came to be called family farms. They were to be linked not by rules of custom or an autocrat's decrees but by market exchange.

In the U.S. system, advocated so enthusiastically by Thomas Jeffer-son, the family unit has consisted only of husband and wife and pre-school or school-age children. It is noteworthy, though, that the indi-vidual farm family of today, even as its extended-family antecedent, has dual status as both a social and a productive economic unit.

Not so with the family in cities. If the urban family is in fact a ves-tige of rural family structure, it is in jeopardy. As it becomes more dis-tantly removed from its agrarian precursor it encounters more danger of collapse. The ties that have bound members of a rural family are weak or absent in cities. The urban family finds it almost impossible to dream up obligations equivalent to a farm youngster's having to feed the chickens or milk the cow lest there be no eggs or milk.

Market Exchange. Throughout history market trading was seldom ab-sent but it usually was confined to a very restricted sphere. It took place between the chiefs of the large units, or among royalty; it was not common within the units. Century upon century of evolution was necessary before anything close to a market economy developed.

In Western Europe, the earliest local markets for farm produce arose more or less accidentally. They were confined to selling whatever surplus remained above producers' own needs. As agriculture became more productive market trading naturally increased.

Market exchange was built into an agricultural system in the New World. As medieval Europe's feudal agriculture was disavowed and replaced by family farms, market trading performed the functions that formerly were the province of overlords.

The saga of emergence of a market system for agriculture deserves fuller telling later, as a subject of its own.

Land and the Work Ethic
As also was suggested in Chapter 1, some of our moral values are often credited to our agrarian tradition. The work ethic is an example. It surely is true that land will produce only insofar as it is worked. More perhaps than any other religion, Christianity endorses work, or even glorifies it. The work ethic has been a central doctrine of Christianity at least since St. Augustine.

Land and the Division of Surplus Value
It would be easy to choose those human philosophies that we regard favorably and enshrine them in agrarianism because, developmentally, the human race survived in an agrarian setting before it devised something more elaborate and more productive.

Agrarian societies were by no means universally beneficent. They may have given rise to the work ethic, but unless some other ethic was also accepted that impulsion was applied mainly to slaves.

Surplus Value. To understand why agrarian systems could be so unfair (by our standards) it is necessary to go back and reconsider the first and fifth characteristics of land. Land is intrinsically an inherited social resource rather than a man-made private one. And land yields variable returns to the labor or other input applied to it—some land barely enough for the cultivator's subsistence, other land a big surplus.

To whom does that surplus belong? This is the issue that above all others makes land and agriculture a battleground of social conflict. The old nobles and kings laid claim to the surplus, and fought among themselves to get it. Ever since, class structure has entered into the economics of the division of the produce, particularly the surplus produce of land.

Doubtless the elders of the early agrarian units were torn between imposing a comparatively stratified or an egalitarian class structure. Very often the former prevailed, as duties were assigned and rewards apportioned according to class distinctions. To this day it seems almost impossible to pierce the dividing lines between classes, so that one part of the population is not doomed to servile labor while the highest stratum lives in luxury. Reduced to essentials, this is what the widespread petition for "agrarian reform" of agriculture in various nations is about.

Now that most kings have been deposed, and where the landed aristocracy is not in complete control, at least part of the surplus value in agriculture is recovered for society in one of two ways. If land remains in the hands of the social unit rather than being privately held, it is captured according to whatever terms of leasing are imposed. If land is privately held, a tax is levied. The general principle of taxation is that the least yielding land in cultivation shall pay no tax or at most a nominal one. Other tax rates are to be proportional to productivity. Taxes reclaim for the benefit of everyone some of the productivity implicit in the fertile loam that the seas or volcanoes deposited eons ago. In addition, appropriately calculated tax rates tend to guide land into its socially most advantageous use.

Insofar as taxes reclaim only part of the return from supermarginal productivity, the rest becomes rent. In economic terms this is a factor share. It is also sometimes called unearned income. In owner-operator (family) farming, the operating farmer keeps this part of income. But in tenancy the owner claims it. In this difference lies much of the dispute over who will own and control farming, to be discussed in a later chapter.

Rent as Residual Return, and Capitalized Land Value

Insofar as the return to privately held land is not taxed away and remains as rent, it becomes capitalized into value of the land. Not only current net return is so capitalized; anticipated return in the future is also capitalized. A second dimension is that future changes in land values themselves can be anticipated in the price buyers are willing to pay for land.

At the mid-1970s, when rent to land and its capitalized value had risen so steadily, an awesome economic principle was almost forgotten: that rent is a *residual* return. It is what is left after all costs are met. When the price of farm products is high relative to operating costs, rent is large. When the price margin is narrow, rent is small. Rent thus is highly levered; it magnifies whatever happens to cash prices and costs. It is the whip on a lash, the end of a teeter-totter.

Rent can go up, as it did in the early 1970s.

It can also go down.

When rent goes down, the price of land goes down too.

An important point follows. A drop in rent and land price does no harm to society. If the reduction accompanies cheaper food to consumers, society may be better off. It obviously plays havoc with the financial position of recent buyers of land, particularly if they are heavily in debt. Their equity can disappear overnight.

Much of the economics of agriculture thus is the economics of how future returns are capitalized into land values. If returns go up, huge capital gains can be realized. If returns go down, losses are incurred.

Sight should not be lost of the difference between what is fundamental and what is ancillary or even superficial. Agriculture's productivity counts for most. The distribution of rewards from productivity is important too. But the speculative game of guessing what net returns will be in the future, and basing one's investments on those guesses, is a different matter. It is pure gambling. It ought to be recognized as such.

Land and the Beginnings of Economic Theory
The notion that a surplus value arises from all supermarginal land has stimulated economic and political theorizing in several directions.

In ancient times, when a powerful sovereign levied away surplus value the revenue supported his armies and his luxuries. But when industrialization began, clever thinkers pointed out that the surplus value from agriculture could finance capital investment for new industry. This was the appealing, exciting doctrine enunciated by the French Physiocrats in the middle of the 18th century.

The Soviet government in our century combined the old and the new as it drained agriculture's surplus, even viciously, to fund its new industry.

American farmers still complain that the countryside has financed the city. Populist farmers of our West have long said that they underwrote the urban splendors of the East.

Land and "Diminishing Marginal Returns." The principle of surplus value made yet another contribution to economic thinking. According to the fifth characteristic of land, when successive "doses" of a variable input such as labor are added to land a smoothly curving pattern of return is revealed. The curve of increasing and decreasing marginal physical returns is as artistically attractive as it is mathematically manipulative.

This phenomenon took on more dramatic meaning when later technology introduced myriad industrial inputs to agriculture. The economics of a (partially) industrial agriculture belongs in the next chapter, not here. What is worth noting here is the teaching value of the demonstrated principle. When thinkers saw how farm production responds to variable inputs, they drew lessons that they then applied to new nonfarm industry—in fact, to much of the economy. Most general economists of today would scorn to admit how much has been learned from the demonstrated economics of agriculture. Yet a capital good as a fixed asset, about which they write so much, is analogous to land. Variable inputs are the equivalent of fertilizer and a farmer's labor in applying it. Surplus value is called not rent but quasi rent.

The socialists picked up the cue. Marx pondered surplus value at length and decided that hardworking laborers really contributed it. (When people work on land to produce a surplus, truly, to whom can it be credited? Perhaps to the creating Deity.)

Land has provided many lessons to be taught all who will learn. Not least is a set of coherent economic relationships that have been converted to apply to an entirely different kind of economy, that of urban industry. Economists of the industrial age may hesitate to declare their intellectual debt, but it nevertheless is owed.

NOTES
1. John Hicks, *A Theory of Economic History* (Oxford: Clarendon Press, 1969).

The singularly most significant element of American economic development was the interaction between agriculture and nonfarm industries. —LUTHER TWEETEN

3 THE (PARTIAL) INDUSTRIALIZATION OF AGRICULTURE

When some clever aborigine fashioned a crude ax or hoe to help him cultivate plants or raise animals he introduced nonfarm resources into farming.

He began a trend that has continued ever since. It has seldom been interrupted. Employing nonfarm resources in producing food and fiber is the essence of what we now call the technology of farming. In broader language, it is the industrialization of agriculture.

Another way to look at it is to say that our agriculture has gone through "development" and is now "developed." These are laudatory words. According to this terminology the United States, Canada, Australia, and Western Europe now fortunately have a developed agriculture. Third World countries lack that blessing. We weep for them. We also spend a lot of money and send many scientists globe-trotting in order to help those countries develop their agriculture.

In developed agriculture many kinds of materials and services are utilized. One simple division is between those that relieve human labor and therefore make the remaining human effort many times more effective; and those that add to productivity of land. A third category might be added. It would include everything that improves productivity of livestock and poultry, too often forgotten. Vaccines and feed additives are examples.

Sometimes knowledge is separated from materials. The word "technology" has itself become ambiguous. It is variously interpreted in terms of technique and of materials used. Fortunately, this word game need not be played. Techniques and materials have come into agriculture as an unmatched pair. Although different, neither is of any

19

value without the other. So no distinction will be made here. We will look upon nonfarm inputs and research knowledge about them as a single package.

Industrialization has given agriculture a new look and new productivity but has not wholly transformed it. Not until the agrarian base is totally displaced will that be possible, and that will not happen in the foreseeable future. On the contrary, the present trend in developed agriculture is to swing back slightly from relying so heavily on such nonfarm materials as fuel and chemical fertilizer, owing to their sharply higher prices. The corollary is to hark more to protecting and conserving that vital agrarian base, productive farmland.

If through magic invention atomic power should someday convert carbon, hydrogen, and nitrogen from rock and air directly into food, provisioning of human beings would become entirely industrial. Until then we are stuck with the erratic biology of plants and animals in a partially industrialized agriculture as the way to keep ourselves alive.

THE POSITIVE ASPECTS OF INDUSTRIALIZATION
Industrialization of U.S. agriculture is not only partial but mixed in its effects. In some ways it has been an unrivaled boon to farmers and the nation—and indeed, because it increases our export capacity, to much of the world.

It also has its drawbacks. They should not be denied.

The better and poorer features will be recounted briefly. It is worth reminding ourselves that both are present.

Relief of Drudgery in Farming
Hand labor on farms is not fun. Some tasks are backbreaking. Others bring exposure to all extremes of weather. Not a few are brutish in their demands for muscle without craft satisfaction. Physical danger is not absent. In spite of the heralded joys of working in God's fresh air and sunlight, injury and illness are frequent in farming.

Industrialization brings mechanical power to farms. It relieves most muscular labor. It permits more work to be done in relative comfort. Some tractors even have air-conditioned cabs!

It does not end all dullness, nor all danger. Safety in farming has hardly been improved. A mechanical corn picker may be safer than a cutting sled, but scarcely more so than cutting corn stalks with a bladed knife. It is no credit to the tractor industry, or to farmer customers, that federal legislation was necessary before rollbars would be attached to tractors.

Freeing Farmers for Other Employment
In the parade of tributes to technology in agriculture the highest tribute is that it freed farmers for employment elsewhere. Erstwhile farmers

manpowered urban industry and there helped produce the shower of industrial products and professional services that has made life in our nation so materialistically splendid.

The language about "freeing" farmers is nevertheless deceitful. Farmers were pushed off the land more often than they were enticed away from it. In the Elizabethan England of the enclosure period, farmers were detached from land faster than new industry could absorb them. Unemployed, unsheltered men tramped the countryside. Many did a little pilfering. Some were apprehended as vagrants and went to the gallows.

Even in our generation, not a few farmers have moved from farm to city employment under the threat of foreclosure. They did not feel "freed."

On the whole, the process of industrialization of Western economies was not pleasant nor even neutral. It was painful, achieved at high human cost.

But the outcome cited so often, that thereby the productivity of a nation was increased marvelously, is correct.

Reciprocity: The Farmer's Share

As farmers' own new technology sped industrialization, which in turn produced more total wealth, the question arises as to how well farmers themselves fared.

In a sense of reciprocity, they might be expected to share fully. Whether they have done so is one of the big issues in the farm policy debates of our century. The debate has not ended.

But a paradox arises. Who has profited most, the farmers who remained on the land, or those who took off and went to the city? The paradox does not end with the question of relative gains. It reaches to the fact that those who remained benefited because others left. In a sort of echoed reciprocity, farmers now farming can give credit to those of their former fellows who did not remain in farming but went to the city. Because some left, those who stayed live better.

Another Reciprocity: Increased Productivity of Farmers

Of and by itself, draining of labor from agriculture reduces agricultural production. Neither in the United States nor elsewhere have workers so overcrowded the land that their displacement sustains gross output.

Yet we say, so glibly, that "development" of agriculture, interpreted to mean partial industrialization, does wonders for agricultural "productivity."

The idea of productivity deserves more responsible analysis than it usually receives.

When farmers went to the city to work in factories, they did not produce only goods for urban people including the urban rich. Some of them turned out tools and fuels to go back to the farm. Those farmers-turned-factory workers thus compensated for their departure by making work easier and more yielding for their onetime compatriots.

The farmer equipped with a new tractor then produced more than one with a spade.

To what or whom should the greater output per farmer be credited? It's like the hoary story that inasmuch as water is common to all intoxicating beverages it must be the intoxicant. The farmer is involved in all man-and-machine combinations in farming. Does he therefore get the credit for his greater production?

It was suggested in Chapter 2 that land rent should be credited to God. Perhaps the farmer's extra output from using a tractor should be attributed to the tractormaker, or the inventor.

Still Another: Increased Productivity of Farm Land

Giving farmers more tools so that fewer could do the work does not of itself add to the total production of U.S. agriculture. Labor substitution is not what adds to total output. It is land substitution that does so.

However, the term land substitution is almost a misnomer. Practices of using more fertilizer, pesticides, and similar inputs amount to land complementarity as much as to land substitution.

But this comment only opens the argument. It does not end it. For there is an intercomplementarity and intersubstitution with human labor. Farmers add nitrogen fertilizer with a drill to keep from having to spread animal manure—which requires more work.

For now, let savants argue the semantics. There is a part of technology in agriculture that of itself adds to productivity of land and therefore to total output. We will consider combined effects later.

Land-substitution technology takes two forms. One is the replacement of farm-produced power by petroleum fuels. When horses and mules gave way to gasoline- or diesel-powered tractors, tens of millions of acres that had produced oats and hay for those workstock became available to produce food and fiber for human beings.

The second is mainly the application of chemicals in agriculture. These increase yields per acre. At the pinnacle is commercial fertilizer, particularly nitrogen. According to USDA estimates, nitrogen fertilizer alone now contributes at least 30 percent to grain yields of the U.S. Midwest.

To land-substituting technology as such can be added increased efficiency in converting the feed crops and pasture produced on land into livestock products for consumers. Progress has not been as dramatic in livestock as in crops. Nevertheless, various materials and services coming from nonfarm industry have increased the quantity and quality of livestock and poultry foods our consumers enjoy.

The time has come in this account for a note of apostasy. Conventional wisdom has it that the technology called land substituting adds enormously to the gross output of U.S. agriculture.

It may do so. It may not. Or—this is the likely answer—it may add less than it is given credit for.

The nub of the argument is the labor substitution that accompanies land-substituting technology. Fertilizers and pesticides are applied by machine. They let one farmer cover vast territory. But he does not cover it very well. Further, mechanized farming is increasingly confined to terrain that accommodates large equipment. It is really a land-wasting technology. If instead of using industrial machinery mounted on rubber tired wheels the United States were to adopt Japanese style farming, cultivating intensively every pocket of productive land, what would happen to total output? The guess offered here is that it would climb significantly.

Although labor-intensive methods would increase gross farm output, its main consequence would be the one highlighted several pages back: it would rob urban industry of its workers, and reduce industrial production.

So we end with the same proverb enunciated before. The magic of technology in agriculture spares farmers backbreaking labor and man-powers our industrial machine; it may, on balance, add little to gross farm output. Farm technology gives us more autos, air-conditioned houses, and guns. It may or may not give us more bread and butter.

PRODUCTIVITY MEASURES FOR A PARTIALLY
INDUSTRIALIZED AGRICULTURE

Some progress has been made in measuring the productivity of an agriculture that puts to work not just man and land, but many other resources too.

Productivity in Terms of Nonfarm Resources

It is agricultural chauvinism to look at productivity in agriculture only in terms of output per unit of farm resources engaged, that is, per farmer or per acre. Why should the farmer think that he and his land alone account for the achievements of modern agriculture? It was suggested earlier that at least the tractor manufacturer should get some recognition. So should lots of other people.

The harsh fact is that the farmer, though still essential, is becoming an ever smaller part of the total food production and distribution complex. It does not disparage the performance given by the hardy tiller of soil or tender of cows to recommend a little modesty.

Conceivably, the lion's share of credit for productivity in U.S. agriculture properly goes to the nonfarmers in the system. These are not just tractor builders but also miners of iron ore and phosphate rock, chemists, researchers, teachers, merchandisers, and dozens of others.

There is a reason for past underappreciation. Nonfarm inputs were so available! During many years most nonfarm resources were regarded as plentiful. They reached agriculture at comparatively low cost. Over a long period prices for petroleum fuels and chemical fertilizer either were stable or lagged behind the general inflation in the economy.

Literally, agriculture drew on those resources as though they came from a well that would never run dry.

Events of the 1970s, which surprised farmers as much as other citizens, tell us convincingly that the well is not bottomless. Some oil wells have in fact been pumped dry. Mines of metal ores are gradually being emptied. In the 1970s Americans have been shocked into realizing that many of the resources on which their prosperity is based are depletable, and are being depleted. Many are used in farming.

To farmers themselves the visible manifestation thus far has been an increase in the prices they must pay for nonfarm inputs. In addition, at a few times in some localities farmers found fuel and fertilizer hard to buy. At the time of writing this essay, physical shortages had eased but the lesson had been learned of how quickly the scene can change. The supply line for oil and steel and potash rock is a tenuous one.

Honest Measures of Farm Productivity

An accounting for the output of today's farms must be expressed in terms of nonfarm as well as farm resources used. If production is to be related to labor, its ratio should be in terms of total labor, direct plus indirect. Professor Folke Dovring of the University of Illinois has protested omitting nonfarm labor. He has even estimated statistically how much manpower goes into producing the machines, fuel, and scientific knowledge that agriculture draws on (1). Not even professional economists have wanted to listen! They prefer to calculate fictitious ratios of how many people are supported per worker on farms. The figures may seem to make farmers look like heroes but it is equally true that it casts them as ingrates.

The U.S. Department of Agriculture, to its credit, has for a number of years computed aggregative indexes of farm productivity in terms of total inputs. The inputs include all resources drawn on, farm and nonfarm together. A technical question may be raised as to whether the price weights induce a bias over time. The effort is nevertheless commendable, however approximate the results may be.

The USDA indexes tell a surprising story. The ratio of output to input advanced slowly during the 1960s, jumped sharply at the turn of the decade, then leveled out in the 1970s.

Perhaps still another kind of productivity index is now needed. Perhaps we ought to measure farm production in terms of *non*farm inputs alone.

If some nonfarm materials are due to become ever scarcer, attention may focus on how effectively they are used. Energy could be our scarcest input—energy for motors, for electric power, for manufacturing nitrogen fertilizer. If so, economy in using it will be mandated. I have proposed that we begin to calculate the ratio of agricultural production to quantity of fossil-fuel energy consumed. Bushels of corn per million BTUs of petroleum? The idea is not outlandish.

THE NEGATIVE ASPECTS OF INDUSTRIALIZATION
Unmixed blessings are few in the universe. Partial industrialization of agriculture is not one. It has its negative aspects, its drawbacks. Some are minor. Others are frightening.

Industrial Regimentation
Regimentation may be too harsh a term but partial industrialization has put agriculture under tremendous pressure to organize itself systematically and methodically. Such is the industrial model. Processors and distributors of farm products follow that model. Market firms want farm products of dependable quantity and quality delivered at regular intervals.

Farmers have their own orderliness but it lies in the discipline of accommodating the variableness of nature, not of fulfilling production quotas.

It is in this difference that the Russians run into trouble. Many years ago they began to industrialize their agriculture with vicious earnestness. They still declare their goals and quotas. After a half century they cannot harmonize the conflict between methodical planners and coquettish nature. Some goals remain unfulfilled and others are abandoned. In frustration the Soviet hierarchy has allowed vegetable farms to harvest their crops when ready and sell them for whatever price they can get!

In our United States some market firms declare that they want to integrate farming with their processing in order to be assured of a regular and quality-controlled supply. There is no reason to suppose they would be any more successful than the Russians. A meat wholesaler was about to enter cattle feeding in order, so he said, "to make all beef lower-third Choice." When it was explained that it is impossible to feed to that close specification he dropped the idea.

A Managerial Revolution
Not just Russians and agribusiness firms run into trouble. Farmers do too.

Industrialization creates for farmers what Paarlberg calls a managerial revolution. He has in mind not simple shifts such as from feeding a horse to fueling a tractor. Those changes farmers can manage. He stresses more the technical complexity of managing so much capital, of learning precision in handling chemicals under environmental rules, and of conforming to laws in hiring farm labor (2).

Another aspect of the managerial revolution is the sharply increased financial risk. It is an aspect that is particularly not appreciated by farmers.

The greater risk comes about because so many of the costs in industrialized farming are cash costs.

Early in this century only a quarter to a third of expenses in farming were current cash expenses. The farmer had to buy machinery, twine, harness, some feed supplements, perhaps some superphosphate. The petroleum products he bought were kerosene for lanterns, harness oil, and axle grease. He raised the feed for his horses, cows, and hogs. Manure from them, not nitrogen fertilizer, returned fertility to the soil.

Industrial techniques plus more specialization of enterprise that separates livestock from feed crops force the farmer to buy more of his supplies now. He may also incur sizable interest charges on the credit used for their purchase. So three-fourths to four-fifths of all expenses are now cash. The financial hazards of farming have multiplied accordingly.

Industrialized Overproduction?
During the years when agriculture was producing beyond market requirements and pushing prices downward, was its new industrial technology at fault?

Some critics said it was. The point was not that new technology was undesirable, but that it came too fast and too erratically. It therefore constantly threatened to undermine the price and capital-value structure.

Supporting evidence is that in the 1970s when industrial inputs suddenly became scarcer and more costly, production stopped surging upward. Coincidence does not prove causation; perhaps bad weather restrained output. But on the whole we can conclude that when new industrial technology comes in too big doses, prices and incomes to farmers may not be sustained.

Industrial Cycles in Farming
Partial industrialization can cause problems for agriculture in another way. Some industrial materials are capital goods that last a while. Even chemical fertilizer persists a few years. If farmers go crazy in increasing productive capacity during good times, the forthcoming larger output can bring a break in prices and ruin to farmers.

The expanded output and reduced prices can last until the overbuilt capacity is absorbed or liquidated. The situation may swing to the other extreme, which also will persist a while, completing a cycle.

Thus does industrialization of agriculture bring the familiar dreaded industrial-type cycles with it. They are most conspicuous in livestock and poultry.

Ah, but proponents of industrializing agriculture tell us that industrial style management will be so professionally skilled that it will eliminate all such problems. The promise is patently false. Industrial management has not stopped cycles in manufacturing industry. Nor has it done so where it has been extended to farming via vertical integration. The integrated broiler industry, for example, has displayed rhythmic expansions and contractions more devastating than those of the years when undisciplined farmers were in charge. The ultimate irony is that integrated broiler producers have sought methods, both visible and, allegedly, clandestine, to cartelize their businesses so as to stabilize production and price (see Chapter 11).

Social Consequences of Industrialization

Loudly proclaimed but still disputed are the effects of the industrialization of agriculture on the people involved—those displaced from farms, and those who remained.

The charge is made with some persuasiveness that substitution of machines displaced workers in farming faster than they could be absorbed in new jobs in new (city) surroundings. Millions of farmers who went to the city seeking to better themselves did not do so. Some languished there. Others returned to the country.

A more poignant consequence may be devaluation of skills. In the kitchen, cake mixes and frozen foods have been said to cost cooks their own and others' esteem. Who now toasts a farmer who can build wheat shocks that withstand a gale or train a horse to pull a corn cultivator without stepping on a single plant?

It is alleged that where farming communities have lost too many people the local business, social, educational, and religious institutions have been damaged. Some small towns have disappeared from Rand-McNally geographies. Even the Post Office gave up on them.

Much has been written on these subjects. They are mentioned here as reminders that social consequences of industrialization of agriculture cannot be dismissed.

Regional Favoritism in Industrialization

Still another indirect cost of industrializing U.S. agriculture is the damage done to those areas that are not well suited to new industrial techniques.

A legion of examples could be cited. Probably the most familiar is moving cotton out of the Southeast, where much human labor was engaged in raising lint on red clay slopes. It went to the flat land of Texas and California where machines could do it all.

Because the point is well known this mention is sufficient.

It is worth also noting, though, that if agriculture in the future must back away from industrialization, previous regional relocation may be reversed to some degree.

INDUSTRIALIZATION AND FARM POLICY

Two sweeping observations draw this chapter to a close.

One is that its industrial features bear heavily on policy for agriculture. Although policy as such will be discussed later, several thrusts can be sketched.

—The financial risks in a more industrial agriculture have contributed to pressures for group protection against those risks including, notably, government programs to underpin prices and incomes.

—Insofar as a traditional proprietary system of farming ("family farming") is retained, a need arises for

    (a) technically oriented research and education to equip farmers to use the new technology. Therein have originated agricultural experiment stations and extension services.

    (b) marketing services that make it easier to give at least some regularity and dependability to the supply of farm products.

—Towering over all else is the question of what kind of structure of agriculture is to prevail in the future. Its agrarian features tend to keep farming in independent units. Its industrial features militate the other way. Which direction will it go?

The Alarm: Vulnerability to Scarcity of Materials

The second concluding statement warns of the consequence of costlier industrial materials.

Industrialization of agriculture came about during a period of absolute confidence in the availability of the materials on which it was based. Although they numbered many, basic to all were the fossil fuels for energy and the metals. It is inevitable that those materials will become ever scarcer and more costly. Adjustments to their scarcity will be to search for substitute materials of industrial origin; to divert some items, notably fuel, away from less essential uses and to farming (perhaps by decree); and to compensate by changing cultural practices in farming. The last named might involve developing drastically new kinds of germ plasm, such as a leguminous corn. This topic too deserves separate discussion. Attention is called here to remind of its relevance to the overall subject of the industrialization of U.S. agriculture.

NOTES

1. Folke Dovring, *Labor Used in Agricultural Production. An Attempt at a Fresh Approach to Productivity in Agriculture,* Dept. of Agr. Econ., AERR–62, (Urbana: Univ. of Ill., April 1962).
2. Don Paarlberg, *American Farm Policy* (New York: Wiley, 1964), p. 39.

God, who hath given the world to men in common, hath also given them reason to make use of it to the best advantage of life and convenience. —JOHN LOCKE

4 COVETED LAND

In Chapter 2 land was treated as an agricultural resource.

Land is that. It is also much more. Land is a site. It is a site for the foundations for office buildings and private homes and industrial plants. It provides trackways for trains, roadways for trucks, and landing strips for aircraft. Armament is installed on land, as is the armor that defends against others' armament. People play on land: it offers opportunity for recreation.

Surface land is also the means of access to other resources, such as buried minerals, and water.

Because human beings are held down by the pull of gravity and move mainly in horizontal direction, land is significant as provider of space. Countless studies have shown that humans, like all animal life, require some arena for movement. Solitary confinement is properly regarded as about the worst punishment that can be imposed on an evildoer.

For all these reasons land is coveted outside agriculture.

With a few big exceptions, land does not have special qualities controlling its use. Some land sought for recreation is not well suited for farming. The wilderness and the mountains that carry appeal for many outdoorsmen do not accommodate the machines with which farming is done. But these happy circumstances are exceptional. Hundreds of millions of acres of land are attractive both for farming and for one or more nonfarm uses.

Competition among uses of land is explained not so much by fertility of soil but by water and topography. In humid and irrigated areas crops grow best and that is also where most people live. Furthermore, not only farmers prefer the level areas; so do builders of homes and industrial plants and airports and military bases.

The unique economics of land also helps explain why land is

coveted. Because land is of fixed supply and a residual claimant to its variable returns, it generates rent. Landholding is sought in order to receive rent.

When the legal system is designed for the purpose, rights to land can be bought and sold. Except as inflation or deflation adds to or subtracts from it, capitalized value of anticipated rental income becomes the price paid. Use of land is then determined by the highest bid price.

Seldom, however, is that system allowed to operate unrestricted. The natural monopoly land possesses leads to certain restrictions on its use. Almost everywhere, laws protect water-access and watersheds. Eminent domain gives priority to location of roads and schools.

NONFARM COMPETITION FOR FARMLAND FOR NONFARM USES

Our concern here is confined to how the coveting of land affects a policy for agriculture. In a sense the contest for land and the terms of making it available (or unavailable) are basic to all else in the economics of agriculture. The contest for land results in some net loss of acreage to farming use each year. More important, however, is how current prices of land as well as tax assessments are affected. Both hold much meaning to farming.

To date, nonfarm competition for farmland has encroached persistently on the domain of land for farming. It is not that the rate of loss is so great. Although much is said about the million acres of land that move from farming into nonfarm uses each year, only about a third of it is arable land. Matched against an inventory of perhaps 350 million acres of readily available plow land, statistically the loss rate is not so alarming.

But that one-third million acres is not average land. Some is very good farmland. Nearly all is advantageously located. It is not land in Montana and New Mexico; it is near cities, and usually also close to existing transport. Over a few years the social harm from relentless despoiling of fertile farmland can be considerable.

Until recently most of the encroachment of nonfarm upon farm use of land was helter-skelter, unplanned. Suburban housing developers have mainly just selected pockets of low priced land. Only recently have suburban communities begun to protect themselves against unplanned development that scars the countryside and creates new public costs for schools and roads.

Nonfarm Speculative Demand

Having said that, we turn to the pricing aspect of nonfarm coveting of farmland. It permeates more and is harder to deal with.

It originates in the fact that wherever farmland carries the potential of moving into nonfarm uses, it also carries a valuation reflecting that potential. Thereupon a speculative demand springs up. Speculative buyers roam the countryside. They sniff for bargains where an unwary farmer will succumb to a purchase offer that exceeds the value of that land to him for farming. They buy a little. They give a speculative price boost to much.

Speculative valuation of land above its value for farming could be relatively innocent were it not for tax policies. If no special law interposes, and if assessors do their job as they are supposed to, speculative value of real estate gets built into its assessment for tax purposes. Farmers who own land that is so valued and so assessed then find themselves billed for taxes that overstate its earning power in farming. The result is to add to the pressure for selling out.

Farmers' Response

What has been sketched thus far is part and parcel of one of the most pervasive elements in the present policy picture. It reflects a basic element in current farm policy. It is the threat posed by the huge nonfarm part of the economy to invade, assimilate, and make over the farming sector and the rural community.

Farming and the rural community stand in danger of losing their identities.

But nonfarm pressure to encroach on farmland is only half the story. The other half is farmers' response. It in turn exemplifies a second basic principle in farm policy, namely, the difference between individual and group interests of farmers. Sometimes what seems good to the individual considered by himself is not good for the group. It may not even be good for the individual once group effects begin to be felt. This principle will be echoed several times in later chapters.

Farmers may respond to the threat of nonfarm usurpation of farmland by self-enrichment capitulation: Let the individual "get his"; sell the land to the highest bidder; give no thought to what happens to the land or the community. This carries the individual interest, if not to its ultimate, then almost there.

The other route is to develop land policies that bring some order to the forces determining use of land. These divide roughly into those relating to taxes, and those using direct controls of some sort.

This brief essay will not dig into the full repertoire of land policies that are available. It will only review a few policy directions for illustration.

Differential Assessment

A recent innovation in tax policy is that of differential assessment. It is now in use in a number of states. It recognizes a potential difference between value of farmland for farming vs. for other use (usually developmental). In differential assessment farmers can petition to have their farmland assessed for taxation according to its farming rather than its developmental value. When this is done they can farm as long as they wish without bearing extra tax cost. They can then sell at their convenience to the highest bidder, developmental or otherwise.

Some states have inserted a recapture clause in their differential assessment law. It requires that farmers who sell out for development must repay the forgiven part of their tax going back about five years. Usually the clause is added during legislative debate. City legislators, not farmers' spokesmen, ask for it.

In broad outline differential assessment may be said to contribute to both better equity and improved land use. Farmers who farm land pay less tax than owners of development land, and an incentive is created to keep land in farming. If recapture is included the case for the law is strengthened.

Nevertheless, the experience thus far throws some doubt on whether differential assessment fulfills even its modest promise. One reason has nothing to do with the law itself. Some farmers, sensing that their state's new differential assessment law would let them ask for concessions, found on checking the records that their land carried a figure far below the market value. Local assessors had lagged in reassessing. Farmers' instant reaction was to let a sleeping dog lie.

A second cause for some loss of confidence is that differential assessment has been utilized about as freely by developer owners of land as by farmers. Particularly when their law contains no recapture clause developers become farmers pro tem. They buy land, scratch it enough to classify as farmers, and apply for tax concessions.

A case can be made that it is in the long-run interest of farmers as a group to attach the recapture clause to a differential assessment law. It may discourage developers who masquerade in overalls. It does no harm to the farmer who genuinely wants to stay on the land.

But apart from varying local circumstances differential assessment probably cannot do much to keep good farmland in farming. At best it will only slow the rate of loss. Some critics doubt it does even that; they say the law works primarily to subsidize speculation. Unless it is effective it does not relieve inequity between the farmer who sells out and the one who stays in farming, and it does little to improve land use in the public interest.

A fair judgment may be that differential assessment is an honest attempt that probably will be replaced by more equitable and more effective methods to guide use of land. But the fast growth of differential assessment laws shows how general is the problem of price and tax systems' effect on allocation of a resource subject to competing uses, namely, land within range of cities.

Land Use Policies
Direct methods of guiding land use have increasingly been employed. They involve some form of govermental acquisition, planning, or zon-

ing. Harshest is outright purchase. It is practiced by the Department of Defense when it wants a new firing range or its Corps of Engineers gets authority to build another dam.

Rural planning and zoning have been adopted slowly. They are local, except that there usually is authority for multicounty agreements.

Idealists who believe land developers should be put under constraint applaud the progress in zoning. Their lenses may be rose tinted, not because zoning is without merit but because both its accomplishments to date and its potential are easily overrated or at least made to appear too simply achieved. Professor Philip Raup of the University of Minnesota believes that rural zoning has thus far done more to protect the local farming "establishment" than to give orderly direction to the development of an area.

Who Gets Capital Gain from Zoning. If equity and resource management are the twin goals of land policy, they come into direct conflict where police power is used to enforce comformity to zoning. Zoning to higher use creates capital gain. It can be very great gain. The gain originates commercially but is channeled by the planning and zoning process, a public action. It then goes to select private recipients. Some become wealthy while their neighbors, excluded from upward rezoning, are not helped. In the longer run the bypassed neighbors may be harmed, as development may bring a higher tax load for public services.

A strong argument can be made for recovering on behalf of the community the extra values that the community itself created by its zoning action. Franklin Reiss is one of several land economists who advance this argument with vigor. Reiss insists that if society would be quicker to tax away the values it itself creates, it could more easily keep farmland in farming and otherwise guide land use. Direct control using the police power would be less necessary and would lead to less opposition (see below). In Reiss's words,

Much, if not most, of the market values we attach to land are the product of society's need for land and not the result of our own contributions. . . .

To the extent [this is true] it would seem logical and just that society should recover, through taxation, at least a part of the value it created. . . .

The opportunities are great for using taxes to achieve land-use goals in the market place rather than through restrictive and perhaps arbitrary regulation.(1)

Decisions on wiser zoning and tax policies including the equity aspects lie farther in the future. To date the most imaginative new devices have been New York's agricultural districts law, New Jersey's transferable development rights, and California's agricultural preserves. Vermont and a few scattered communities have imposed a special tax on capital gains from real estate transfers. These and other schemes must be tried and tested, much time must pass, and a lot of acrimonious debate must be endured before a rational policy can be reached for guiding land use on behalf of all citizens.

Tight Zoning and Seller Monopoly. There is another side to the zoning issue. It relates to developer buyers, and it too involves a question of equity. If zoning is tight enough to confine all new development to prescribed locations, developers would be put in a bind. They would face sellers who enjoyed a zoning-based monopoly. The situation is analogous to a Highway Commission's buying land on which a new highway has been laid out. Just as it has proved necessary for courts to determine fair value of highway land, even so would tight zoning likely lead to judicial rather than market pricing of land that qualified for development. (Pricing of land for sale for right-of-way creates a different inequity in that adjoining land suitable for development can sometimes get a higher price in market sale than the courts allow right-of-way owners.)

Violent Opposition. If some rural communities have adopted at least a mild kind of zoning to avoid the most helter-skelter land development, in some places a local leadership has beat the political drums in opposition to all forms of land use control. Seldom do the spokesmen address the indirect control implicit in tax policies. At some public meetings physical violence has been threatened.

No Easy Escape Route
The basic characteristics of land as fixed in supply and vital to human beings' very survival are powerful.

As population pressure mounts, land will be coveted even more.

And as this happens, the political process will have more say over use of land. It probably will restrain the loss of good farmland to non-farm development. In some fashion the American public will guard the supply of land on which its food is produced.

Although farmers will generally be unfriendly toward some uses of zoning authority, as a group they will not be harmed by wisely chosen policies to stabilize the accessibility, price, and tax rates for farmland.

The first and most basic ingredient of a policy for agriculture is to set the terms by which land is made available to those who farm it.

NOTES
1. Franklin J. Reiss, "Taxation-Land Use Relationships," *Illinois Agricultural Economics,* Department of Agricultural Economics (Urbana: University of Illinois, January 1975), pp. 1, 6.

The biggest issue of agricultural policy is this: Who is going to control the farm policy agenda and what subjects will be on it?
—Don Paarlberg

5 WHO MAKES FARM POLICY?

The interrogatory title to this chapter could be supplemented by other questions:

What is farm policy?

Who are farmers?

Who ought to make "farm" policy?

Perhaps a few negatives should follow. They could be:

There is no such thing as farm policy.

There are not many "real" farmers, and certainly not many who actively engage in policy making.

No one group, least of all farmers, has exclusive policymaking power. Nor ought any one group have it.

The smaller the group the better its chance to get its way politically.

And the clinching negative may well be:

Whoever has political power will deny having it.

THE "WHAT IS FARM POLICY?" ISSUE

Policy issues in farm affairs have been touched on in previous chapters and will be treated in more depth later. It is nevertheless timely to pose the question: What, indeed, is farm policy?

It is a lot of things. In recent years it has been interpreted mainly in terms of price and income supports. This is an unfortunate mistake. Farm policy is much more than that. Yet there are serious problems of definition and we must be on guard against calling farm policy any economic policy that affects farmers. Every national economic policy affects farmers!

At the least, farm policy includes land use policy, marketing policy with respect to both input and product markets, research and education, farm-product aspects of foreign trade policy, structure of agriculture ("who will control?"), and of course price and income policy including any versions that consider special needs of low income farmers.

This capsule definition does not carry farm policy all the way into community development or into food-for-consumers. Admittedly, farm policy decisions affect the rural community. They likewise affect consumers. But boundaries have to be set, and it is better not to try to extend farm policy too far.

In any case the term is loose and limits are a matter of judgment.

WHO ARE FARMERS?

The question of who farmers are is harder to answer than that of what farm policy is.

Farmers are one of the most polyglot groups on the face of the earth. Edward Higbee made the point well a decade and a half ago when he wrote:

American farmers are not one species but many. They may be anything from a weekend hobbyist in Bermuda shorts who raises strawberries for the gang at the office to a corporation with a million acres of land woven by teletype into a transcontinental empire. (1)

To this I have added,

He could have mentioned the small tobacco farmer of the Southeast, clinging to his tiny tobacco allotment as his only protection against both starvation and the cigarette barons who buy his product; or the corn-hog man of the Midwest who bought his land on a shoe-string in 1933 and now has an inflation-boosted equity of $100,000 or more, and conservatism to match . . . and the rancher of coyote country, fiercely proud of his "spread" . . . or the "farm" in California financed with shares of common stock. (2)

And so on, ad infinitum. Which of the above or other categories is a farmer? Are all farmers? If so, how do they arrive at any common political position?

Farmers divide by size. There are many small farmers, few big ones (see Fig. 5.1). Philip Raup, mindful of the pyramid, reminds that "the voting strength in agriculture is at the low end of the income scale while the economic strength is at the upper end." He wonders if U.S. agriculture is drifting into a dual structure. The medium sized and smaller farms possess "some voting strength but little economic muscle." The other sector is "numerically small but economically powerful." Further, "lacking votes and possessing economic power, it finds it increasingly tempting to achieve its goals through the manipulation of the power structure"(3).

Farmers divide by the extent of their interest in farming. Many are, as Higbee said, weekend farmers. Others are part-time farmers,

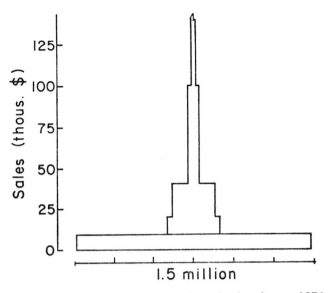

Fig. 5.1.   Number of farms by value of sales classes, 1976

though not all of these are small. Some so-called commercial farmers spend about as much time on off-farm jobs as on the farm. Many retired persons live on farms but depend on their retirement income. Off-farm interests of farmers are so great that in six of the ten years from 1966 to 1975 the farm population received more personal income from nonfarm sources than from farming.

The mental picture of the commercial farmer who gives full time to farming and relies solely on it for his living is appealing. It is politically useful (see below). But it is atypical. That kind of farmer is definitely a minority among the two to three million of our citizens classed as "farmers."

Yet these differences of size and interests are not what most affect farmers' policymaking role. Much more important is the ever higher degree of specialization among farmers. This is the force that fractionates agriculture politically. Diversified farmers of yesteryear felt kinship with their similar fellows. Specialized farmers of today have narrow commodity loyalties. The cash corn farmer identifies with every other cash corn farmer but less with the wheat or cotton producer and scarcely at all with the specialized hog farmer. He is most distant from the hog farmer who runs a big corporate farrowing or feedout operation.

FARMERS IN THE POLITICAL PROCESS

The quizzical lines that opened this chapter and the puzzle of defining farm policy and farmers set the tone for what follows. The whole subject of policymaking is obscure. To many persons it seems mysterious. Although aphorisms are many and accusations abound (such as that a few bosses run the show), by and large most people admit to being confused.

It may seem anomalous but farmers and their leaders, by their pronouncements and tactics, do not clarify but contribute to the haze. They do this if not deliberately then at least routinely.

For the political process is a game. It is a serious game, and at times a deadly one, but it nevertheless is a game. It has strategy with feint, maneuver, and even deception.

Protested Innocence
One part of the game is to avoid revealing one's resources. He who has few pretends to more, and he who has many hides them.

A group that wields power invariably cloaks its actions and denies its success. This rule applies to farmers who come together for political action. Few groups so assiduously protest their political innocence. "We are just a bunch of country boys. You city people will shear us every time." Various versions of this refrain are heard in every state capital and in Washington. They are as strategically sound as they are factually false. Not many pressure groups are as adept in the political process as those that represent farmers.

A few farm organizations, of course, break the rules. Although most take the "we're little lambs" line, a few do not. In the last decade some of the dairy cooperatives chose to go the other route. They brandished their newly won political influence. Their political contributions made the evening TV news. In a sense the dairymen had bad luck in timing, for their exposure came during the Watergate period. But they were brash novices. A few of us had shouted warnings. Retrospectively we are believed (though the lesson may not last).

The Paradox of Denied Dependence
Don Hadwiger points out a companion tactic that is politically instinctive with farmers, and serviceable. It fits with the posture of meekness named above. It is the paradox that farmers proclaim their self-reliance and independence from everyone including government and even at times their scorn for the political process. Yet, apparently oblivious to their chameleon behavior, they are not abashed to call for government aid when they find themselves in trouble.

Their equivocal stance is the more paradoxical because the traditional proprietary farm could not survive in the industrialized economy of our era without some special attention in law.

Hadwiger calls paradox the farmer's "most abundant product." He taunts that "as theologians are grateful for the Trinity, historians and political scientists should be grateful for the American farmer," who fills history with so many instances of paradox. Historical examples are those self-respecting farmers who were the first to rebel against the Republic (in Shay's rebellion) and "rural pragmatists who bit hardest for third parties." Hadwiger adds farm "conservatives who provided the most votes for Socialist and Populist platforms" (4).

Illustrations of paradox have already been cited in these pages. More are to come.

Farmers who ideologically downgrade government asked for and got rural free delivery of mail, the right to form cooperatives and bargaining associations, rural electrification, cooperative credit, auditing of packers who buy their hogs (and now, bonding), semimonopoly privileges in marketing milk and fruits and vegetables, and billions upon billions of public funds spent in their behalf. Every drought brings drought aid, every price break a government purchase program, and so on.

From 1955 to 1975 the federal government paid out $42 billion in direct payments to farmers. It spent $27 billion to finance Food-for-Peace exports, of which only a little was recovered. Price support operations of the Commodity Credit Corporation were another enormous cost. School lunch and other supplementary food programs ran into a large expenditure.

With so much help readily forthcoming, farmers can safely proclaim their ideological conservatism. They can announce their conservative purity even as they take their government check to the bank—or even their private check that is larger because of some government program.

It is all a part of the game that constitutes politics.

The Image and the Scheme

The last of the contrasts to be named here, which also could be called a paradox, is the duality between the good-farmer image that wins so much public sympathy, and the maneuver on particular issues that farm groups engage in as brazenly as any other political body.

Farmers enjoy respect among citizens at large. Their popular image centers on their independent family-farmer status. The farmer is seen as the last of the hardy citizens who alone wrestles with both the vicissitudes of nature and the cupidity of man. That sturdy citizen provisions all of us, and we all are in his debt. This is the picture. It is essentially valid.

Farm politicians are careful to cultivate yet not overexploit that image. It provides a wonderful base for pursuing their bread-and-butter legislative campaigns.

And how do they do the latter? The same as any other self-interest group: they try to find sympathetic spokesmen in the Congress and, for that matter, in the executive branch. They seek out allies. They horse trade.

The most astute pragmatic political leaders try to pull all this off without antagonizing anyone. Why? Because in the game that is American politics, alliances are necessary but are almost always ad hoc. Soybean producers may have one set of allies on the environmental issue today and seek another set for foreign trade politicking tomorrow. Some of today's opponents may be tomorrow's valued confederates. In politics alienation is always to be avoided.

At this point we encounter the grandest paradox of all. It is that the more narrow the issue, the easier it is to win a political battle. This is a paradox because according to conventional wisdom the natural majorities have it easiest, and groups with minority status (including farmers who bewail theirs) have it toughest.

In reality, the more comprehensive an issue the more likely it is that equally sizable groups will be opposed and must be won over or compromised. The big issues are the hardest to manage.

Corn, wheat, and cattle are examples of commodities for which any political issue gets lots of publicity. Tobacco, peanuts, and wool are so small that almost no one worries about them. Furthermore, even generous aid to tiny commodities adds up to few dollars. Therefore tobacco, peanuts, and wool have been treated royally.

THE ROLE OF NONFARMERS IN MAKING FARM POLICY

These last comments introduce an issue that has burned hot in farmers' minds in the 1970s. Farmers say that just about everyone else must be appeased before a farm law can be enacted. In appeasing, farmers complain, they may lose almost all they sought.

The complaint is partly valid, but only for major issues and big commodities. For run-of-the-mine legislative matters, farm spokesmen work hand in glove with the executive branch and committees of the Congress with relatively little exposure and few obstacles.

For big issues political alliances must be formed and political concessions made. Very often, nonfarm political spokesmen (1) set certain minimum conditions that any farm law must meet, and (2) require that farm legislators support specified urban legislation.

In the last decade it has been possible to enact a major farm law only if three conditions were met. Urban legislators specified them. They are:

—More use of direct Treasury payments than of commodity price supports to boost farmers' income. (The reasoning: high supports add to the price of food, but direct payments do not.)

—Limitation to size of individual payments.

—Support of the food stamp program.

All these conditions have in fact been met.

Some years ago Congressman Poage, then Chairman of the Committee on Agriculture of the U.S. House of Representatives, came to the Missouri Governor's Conference on Agriculture to shout at the top of his strong voice that he had voted for rat control in New York City because that was the way he could get a city vote for pest control on Texas ranches. Countless Congressmen and Senators from rural districts have found themselves voting for not only rat control but also various other urban programs. That was the way they won urban votes for farm programs.

The Nonfarm Public and Farm vs. Food Policy

Give-and-take in the legislative scramble does not fully explain whether the urban public has become so sensitive about food supplies and prices that it will virtually convert farm policy into food policy.

During the food price inflation of 1973–75, many farmers thought that was happening.

In a sense all farm policy is food policy, for it affects the supply and price of food to consumers. Consumers and their spokesmen know this.

Yet during all the years prior to the 1970s, consumers scarcely lifted their voice regarding farm programs. The reason was that they were treated rather well and saw no reason to protest. They were not disinterested. They merely were relatively satisfied.

Thus will it ever be. Big harvests, like big dinners, put consumers to sleep. Small harvests, especially when accompanied by strong export demand, are an alarm that wakens them sharply.

Good Will and Wise Politics

The image of the hard working and trustworthy farmer that the nonfarm public still accepts is the biggest single political asset farmers hold.

Years ago the late Karl Brandt, who had been an advisor to President Eisenhower, stated his conviction that "the extraordinary good will which the urban public entertains toward farmers should be treated . . . with utmost respect" (5).

If farmers want to retain political voice, they must truly make sure that they treat urban good will with highest respect. This principle calls for discretion and restraint. It rebukes the clumsy political maneuvering of dairy cooperatives. It calls for a touch of moderation in all demands farm organizations make. It virtually requires that farmers bite their tongues and stay patiently quiet when a few consumers' groups voice their indignation, as they did in the harmless beef boycott of a few years ago. Among other justifications for farmers' self-restraint is that consumers unhappy with prices do not single out farmers from other targets. Very often, according to opinion polls, their anger is aimed mainly at retailers. They scold farmers least of all.

Urban Good Will and the Family Farm

On one policy issue the urban public is almost unanimous. City folks are supportive of the family farm. They may be more so than farmers are.

Just as their basic good will originates in their image of the hard working independent farmer, whom they trust far more than any big corporation, urban voters are favorably disposed toward keeping that kind of farmer.

It will be argued in later chapters of this book that the organizational structure of agriculture is the number one issue in farm policy today. The urban public with its reservoir of good will is a datum of big proportion relative to that issue.

NOTES

1. Edward Higbee, *Farms and Farmers in an Urban Age* (New York: Twentieth Century Fund, 1963), p. 45.
2. Harold F. Breimyer, *Individual Freedom and the Economic Organization of Agriculture* (Urbana: Univ. of Illinois Press, 1965), p. 116. The equity figure could be doubled or tripled now.
3. Philip M. Raup, "Economic, Social, and Political Forces That Will Bear Upon U.S. Agriculture and Welfare of Farmers in Years Ahead," *Central Issues in Agricultural Policy,* Agricultural Experiment Station Special Report 163 (Columbia: University of Missouri, 1974), p. 17.
4. Don F. Hadwiger, "Farmers in Politics," *Agricultural History* 50, No. 1, (January 1976), pp. 156–70.
5. Karl Brandt, "Discussion: Farm Fundamentalism—Past and Future," *J. Farm Econ.* (December 1962), p. 1232.

There is the principle . . . that, inasmuch as land in a prosperous country brings in a constantly increasing income to its owner, apart from any exertion or expenditure on his part, it may and ought to be subjected to special taxation by virtue of that increase.
—JOHN STUART MILL (1873)

6 WHAT FARMERS ARE PAID FOR: PRODUCTION VS. CAPITAL GAINS AS INCOME SOURCES

In the final analysis, whether there is a farm policy and what it consists of will be determined by that big, faceless, amorphous group, the U.S. public.

Citizens holding so much power act more upon general impressions than exact understanding of issues. They form impressions about how well farmers perform and about how adequate their incomes are. They are attentive also to who gets those incomes. On the basis of their impressions they lean favorably or unfavorably toward proposals for farm policy.

Adequacy of incomes and fairness of distribution may well be the touchiest part of all farm policy. Distribution questions involve the wide differences in income received by the few big vs. the many small farmers (see Chapter 5). They involve also the division of income between people who do the work of farming and holders of land. This chapter will be devoted to the second issue. It rose to prominence in the 1970s as so much of total return to farming took the form of capital gain.

Although capital gain traces in part to inflation, it, like rent on land, is an unearned income. Unlike rent it is taxed at a lower rate than earned income. And so long as land stays in a single family, capital gain on it is not taxed at all.

At the mid-1970s the economics of agriculture was not so much the economics of planting and harvesting crops or feeding and milking cows. It was more the economics of capital values and tax rules.

ESSAY 6

FARMING'S CURRENT INCOME FROM PRODUCTION

Farming generates several kinds of income. The income, in turn, goes to several recipients. (The language used here is not the official accounting terminology of the U.S. Department of Agriculture.)

Farming produces a current gross income. This is simply the value of products produced, including any consumed by the farmer's family. It is roughly proportional to the quantity of those products. If the pricing system works well it approximates agriculture's contribution to the national income—to society.

Part of current income goes to pay the cost of purchased inputs including depreciation on equipment, and including also the cost of wages paid to hired workers. These costs are precommitted. They are a preferential claimant.

The rest of current income is divided two ways. Part of it goes to what we usually call labor and management. Strictly speaking it extends to entrepreneurship, including entrepreneurial risk. (This is not the same as longer-term investment risk. The latter is simply gambling. It ought to be recognized as such.)

The other portion of current income is credited to land. At this point begin the explosive issues in distribution of income from farming. How much should go to the work and risk in production, and how much to land? The former is sometimes called earned income. The latter is unearned. The debate has torn societies apart from time immemorial.

Return to labor, management, and risk-bearing is earned income pure and undefiled. A man or woman works and is rewarded. Return to land, called rent in economic language, comes about because land is scarce and of varying productivity. All supermarginal land yields rent. This was explained in Chapter 2.

In the farmer's language rent is recognized as such only if it is paid to someone else (i.e., to a landlord). But in an economic sense there is a rent component to income even if the operating farmer owns the land and therefore keeps it. In fact, one of the important features of owner-operated farming is that the person who does the work gets to keep the rent.

A portion of rent return to land is taxed away. The rest is an income flow. People buy the right to receive that flow. They pay for that right in the price of land.

Land as a Place of Employment

Insofar as land is priced according to its earning power and not anticipated inflation, the numerator in the pricing formula is the current and anticipated rent and the denominator is the wage for which farmers are willing to work.

Land is a base for employment. This obvious and undeniable fact is often overlooked. Farmers in effect bid for the opportunity to be employed. If they buy land to farm, their bid enters into the price they pay. If they lease the land, their bid is in the rental rate, cash or share. It follows that if farmers, including renters, are hard pressed to find employment they will accept lower returns for their labor and the price of land is thereby pushed higher. If the opposite situation prevails land is priced lower.

Until recently in our history land was viewed mainly as a place of employment. The great clamor was not for land from which to receive rent. What was sought was land on which to work and so earn a living for oneself and one's family.

When land was abundant and readily available most of the return from it went to labor, and rent was small. As land becomes scarcer yet farmers need it for employment, rent increases relative to the share of income that goes to labor, management, and risk bearing.

Don Paarlberg has pointed out emphatically that farmers have been willing to underbid their labor services in order to have employment. That is a major explanation why, during so many years, net incomes in farming lagged behind incomes elsewhere. Paarlberg's conclusion is simple: "Low average per capita income in agriculture is a result of the willingness of farm people to offer their labor for a low return" (1).

It follows that the state of industrial employment has much bearing on incomes to farmers. When off-farm employment is booming farmers need not sell their services so cheaply in farming. When off-farm jobs are scarce, farmers necessarily accept subnormal returns for their efforts in farming.

Rising Rents and Owner-Operatorship

How much income goes to labor-management vs. how much to rent has much bearing on who will own and control farming, and especially on whether new younger farmers can hope to be owners.

Owner-operatorship has long been regarded favorably. It is often called the ideal.

As observed above a main feature of farmers' owning the land they farm is that they keep the implicit rental return. It is a part of their total realized income. Scarcely any social question arises. But as the rental portion increases and the price of land goes up, it becomes harder for an operating farmer to own the land he farms. It especially becomes harder for a young farmer to own land. The cost of land is a major obstacle to entry as owner-operator.

Many thoughtful persons have wondered if some kind of special aid will have to be given young farmers if owner-operatorship is to survive. When he was president of the American Farm Bureau Federation Charles Shuman used to say much about this.

A Farm-propertied Class. If operating farmers cannot afford to buy their land, landholding will drift toward a propertied class. Some members will be hereditary farmers. Many others will be nonfarmers.

During the prosperous early 1970s farmers gave nonfarmers tough competition in buying land. Businessmen, lawyers, physicians and other nonfarm investors swooped down on the countryside, looking for tracts of land to buy. They often were spurred by the chance to get a tax break. Yet at the same time established farmers, with their penchant for buying bigger tractors than they need and aided by buoyant incomes, bid vigorously for smaller farms that were put on the market.

Any drop in farm incomes would cut back farmers' ability to compete. And in any case, landholding is very likely to move into a restricted propertied class.

Deficiency Payments as Unearned Income

All this discussion has been confined to return from products sold or consumed at home.

In some years payments by government have been a separate source of current income. Some of these are for value received—for something the farmer has done. An example is reimbursement for part of the cost of building water-conserving dams. Some payments, on the other hand, are strictly supplements to income. They are not a return for actual production but simply a grant. They are unearned income. Indeed, critics of farm price and income programs have lambasted the deficiency payment concept as improper if not immoral.

The defensive rationale for deficiency payments is that farmers who get them have actually produced very well. They may have overproduced. If the market pricing system underrewards thems, deficiency payments compensate. Such is the argument. Profarmer partisans who view deficiency or compensatory income payments in this light do not want to call them unearned income.

We need not debate the merit of a deficiency payment program. It is enough to recognize that in some years farmers get current income from the U.S. Treasury as income supplement, not as direct payment for product sold or service performed.

THE CAPITAL GAINS ISSUE

Deficiency payments and rent thus are two kinds of unearned income. Question about the social ethic of receiving deficiency payments is as new as those payments, but of receiving rent is as old and familiar as the hills.

A third unearned income is old in fact but new in significance. It is the return in agriculture known as capital gains.

The idea that real property tends to rise in value is indeed old. But as a rule the rate of increase has been so slow as to get little attention.

And in U.S. agriculture, insofar as farmers have owned the land, any gain in land value was not conspicuous. Furthermore, it was often viewed as a deserved bonus that compensated for farmers' low current incomes.

The principle has not changed but the magnitude has increased severalfold. In the 1970s, capital gains in agriculture have been huge. Also, they are all tied up with inflation. They get favorable treatment in tax laws, including estate taxes. They are a contentious issue in farm policy.

Size of Agriculture's Capital Gains

A few data will show the magnitude of capital gains in agriculture. Agriculture had substantial capital gains in the 1960s and big ones in the early 1970s. From 1960 through 1976, the value of physical assets in agriculture appreciated $411 billion. Land alone appreciated $350 billion. Net income to farmers from farming, including rent paid to landlords, totaled $325 billion for those years. Thus the return from capital gain exceeded that from current production.

Boom years for capital gains began in 1972. Although much was said about the doubling of net income to $33 billion in 1973, real estate assets increased by $59 billion in that year, and total physical assets by $76 billion. During the five years 1972–76, real estate advanced from

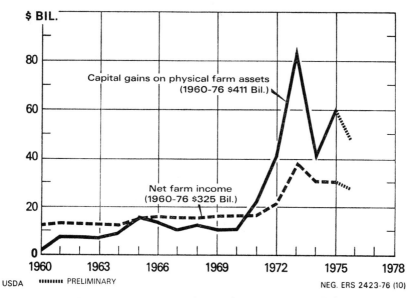

Fig. 6.1.   Farm income and capital gains. Source: **Balance Sheet of the Farming Sector, 1975,** U.S. Dept. of Agr.

$228 billion to $461 billion in value, as it more than doubled. The net income from farming operations was $152 billion in the same years (see Fig. 6.1).

The Nature of Capital Appreciation

Capital value appreciation is so much a part of the current U.S. scene that a few notes follow to explain what it is about. Any capital value is only the estimated worth of claims upon future income. Capital value (i.e., price) of a parcel of land is the worth of anticipated rental return from it. Capital value of stock shares is the discounted earning power of a business firm as a going concern.

In strictest terms, capital value appreciation is confined to gains in value of assets over and above actual costs applied to their improvement. Capital items appreciate or depreciate in value—i.e., in price paid for them—according to changing prospects for net revenue. If net revenue is thought likely to rise, capital values take an anticipatory jump. If revenues are due to fall, capital values will weaken. All this is only a way of describing speculative anticipation of income changes.

Intergenerational Income Transfer. Capital value appreciation gets so much scrutiny because it represents an income that is not only unearned but is transferred from the next generation to the present one. To say it differently, when the present generation realizes a capital gain on an asset by selling it at a higher price, the next generation in effect invests that higher price. Its prospective net income is reduced equivalently. Stated in still other words, appreciation of asset values is unearned only by the present generation. It is earned indeed by the next—unless it defaults.

Social Origin of Appreciation. Appreciation of capital assets gets a going-over for a second reason, namely, that it often arises in some degree of monopolization, whether natural or artificial. Land rises in value, for instance, because a growing population puts pressure on the fixed supply. If society creates the rising value, to whom ought the appreciation go?

Any commercial business that successfully establishes a trademarked product or is a part of a shielded oligopoly wins a boost in its asset valuation. Any other firm wanting to buy into the action (such as a conglomerate on the prowl) will have to pay the higher price.

The Pressure for More Capital Gain. The unearned return represented by capital gain is nectar to the investor. Nothing could be sweeter. It is so delicious that holders of capital assets will do everything possible to get more of it. Not only will they take private routes. They are likely also to create pressure for a public policy that keeps capital values high and rising.

Some salty pundits say that these attitudes and actions go far to account for our relentless inflation.

Inflation in Agriculture's Capital Gain

From the depression low in 1933 to 1977 the average value of farm real estate (land and buildings) in the United States multiplied eighteen times.

Between 1960 and 1977 the price increased more than four times (Table 6.1).

Part of the rise in price of land only reflected inflation. Nevertheless, owning to the growing relative scarcity of land plus anticipated further price increases, from 1960 to 1977 the price advanced almost twice as fast as the cost of goods and services farmers buy (Table 6.1). The price of land quadrupled, the cost of things bought rose 140 percent.

Put another way, if farm real estate prices had risen after 1960 in line with prices paid for goods and services, real estate assets in 1977 would have been worth $315 billion instead of the $461 billion reported for that date. The return due to capital gain, not explained by inflation, amounted to $146 billion (2).

TABLE 6.1.   Index of farm real estate values and of prices paid by farmers for items bought, 1960–77

	Index number of value of farm real estate per acre.[a] 1967=100	Index number of prices paid by farmers for commodities and services, interest, taxes, and wage rates. 1967=100.
1960	68	88
1961	69	88
1962	73	90
1963	77	91
1964	82	92
1965	86	94
1966	93	98
1967	100	100
1968	107	104
1969	113	109
1970	117	114
1971	122	120
1972	132	127
1973	150	145
1974	187	169
1975	213	185
1976	242	199
1977	283	(212)

[a] Land and buildings, on March 1.
Source: Reports of Economic Research Service, U.S. Department of Agriculture.

THE CONSEQUENCES OF BIG CAPITAL GAIN IN AGRICULTURE

To a generation lucking into big capital gains (after its fathers or grand-fathers had suffered losses) it may seem heretical even to raise a question about the desirability of capital gains.

And yet, the whole idea of a capital gain income is a contradiction of all that has been declared as the fundamental value system of U.S. agriculture. Farmers have called themselves the defenders of traditional ethical values. Reward for effort has been their announced creed. Capital gains are the antithesis of reward for productive effort. They are unearned income.

Reduced or Excused Taxes

But that is not the whole of it. Not only are capital gains unearned by productive work but they get highly favorable tax treatment.

Capital gains incur taxes currently at about half the rate paid on earned income. Capital gains taxes on land need not be paid currently. They need not be paid at all if land is bequeathed to descendants and retained by them.

The counter argument is offered that capital gains reflect inflation and therefore should not be taxed at all. But only half the gains between 1960 and 1976 were explained by inflation. Meanwhile, most other tax rates likewise have scarcely been corrected for inflation.

To analyze the various issues of equity in tax policy would take us too far afield. The subject is dropped here.

Capital Gains and Risk of Deflation

Several other aspects of capital gains are worth a line. Asset values, once on an uptrend, are prone to speculative overescalation. They therefore present an extreme hazard of collapsing sometime in the future. High capital values are essentially precarious.

Capital Gains and Misdirected Investment

During a speculative wave in agriculture, better known as a land boom, when funds are invested in the hope of getting further capital gains less money is likely to be spent to increase the productiveness of land. In a social sense, this is misdirected use of investment funds.

The boom of the early 1970s had little land-improvement content. A case can be made that fervent speculation, on balance, actually reduces productivity.

Capital Gains and Pressure for High Price Supports

Even though land is bought in the hope of realizing further capital gain, canny farmers want their current cake too. The farm-policy air of 1976 and 1977 was filled with exhortations to base target prices on "cost of production," which would include an interest allowance on currently inflated land value. First Secretary of Agriculture Butz donned his professional economist's robe to warn against doing so. Then his successor Robert Bergland, a farmer, confined his proposals to a relatively modest 1½ percent allowance for land value. Many farm leaders protested.

Capital Values and Real Estate Taxes
Even more down-to-earth is how speculatively inflated land prices can distort real estate taxes and therefore land use. Most local assessors are conservative about reassessing land prices fully according to the market. But insofar as they follow their local laws and raise assessments they place a tax burden on farmers. Reassessment reflecting speculative values is most likely near metropolitan areas. The result can be to force land out of farming. To avoid that outcome, a number of states have enacted differential assessment laws (see Chapter 4).

Capital Gains and Who Will Control Farming
If agriculture continues to be a capital gains attraction it will move out of the hands of operating farmers. Owner-operatorship as an institution of agriculture will then be doomed.

Farmers want to invest in land as a seat of employment. That object attracts no nonfarmer. Nonfarmers invest primarily in order to receive rent and capital gains.

The more attractive the unearned incomes, the richer will be the class of nonfarm investors who buy land. This rule applies especially to capital gains, for their favorable tax treatment makes them an irresistible lure to high tax-bracket investors.

Likewise, the more favorable the tax treatment given farm estates, including the accrued capital gains tax liability, the more vigorously will wealthy nonfarmers seek farmland investment.

A CAPITAL GAINS TAX POLICY
The rapid-fire comments on capital gains given above should not be translated into a prescription for tax policy on that kind of return, in agriculture or in the economy. A good case can be made for separating the inflationary from the noninflationary aspect of capital gains and treating the latter the same as regular income. Any policy relating to capital gains must deal also with capital losses. This too is a separate subject requiring separate analysis.

A MORAL LESSON
This chapter points as much to a moral lesson as to policy. The author concluded a monthly extension letter that he called a "morality essay" with words that may serve equally well here:

Appreciation of capital values in agriculture has yielded a windfall income to many thousands of farm families who have been in position to cash in on it. We can rejoice in their good fortune.

It promises a paper profit, not yet realized and perhaps not realizable, to two million more. A great many will not get it.

This is the sort of moral situation that poet and priest have deplored since at least Old Testament times. Its benefits are brief and false and confined to a few. Its harm can be excruciating for many, when the bubble bursts.

Moreover, insofar as the liquidating owner cashes in successfully he does so at the cost and risk of the new man buying in. Capital gains to the past generation are a new and burdensome capital cost to the next. And the new capital costs encourage the newly burdened generation to plug for more of the same inflationary policy.

No real wealth is created by a chain letter game, a lottery, or speculation in land. Any nation that tries to build upon such manipulation is headed for trouble. (3)

NOTES

1. Don Paarlberg, *American Farm Policy* (New York: Wiley, 1964), p. 60.
2. Capital gains data from Carson D. Evans and Richard W. Simunek, *Balance Sheet of the Farming Sector, 1975,* U.S. Dept. of Agr., Econ. Res. Serv., Agr. Information Bulletin No. 389, Supplement No. 1, April 1976.
3. Harold F. Breimyer, "Where Money in Farming Comes From," *Economic and Marketing Information for Missouri Agriculture,* Cooperative Extension Service, (Columbia: Univ. of Missouri, September 1975).

My object all sublime
I shall achieve in time—
To let the punishment fit the crime.
                                        —W. S. GILBERT

7 PRICE AND INCOME POLICY FOR AN AGRARIAN AND INDUSTRIAL AGRICULTURE

Price and income programs are not synonymous with economic policy for agriculture but in recent decades they have certainly dominated it.

It is a premise of these essays that farmers are ideological in good times but pragmatic in bad ones. On this premise we can expect price and income issues to reclaim the limelight whenever the euphoria of the mid-1970s ends. In 1977 it seemed about to end.

According to the opening lines of Chapter 6 the basic equation for giving public aid to agriculture has little to do with complicated parity formulas or other mathematics. It is a matter of whether the general public thinks farmers are doing well or badly. Implied in that chapter is that the big capital gains of recent years give farming a reputation for riches. The public will be slow to heed any early claims of poverty and need for help.

Also bearing on citizens' attitudes is whether their image is of an agriculture of modest family farmers or well-heeled big ones. If the former, they will be generous. If the latter, they will be stingy.

On balance, the prospect is that farmers will call for help earlier than the public is willing to grant it.

In any event, price and income programs belong in any treatise on farm policy. The ideas that follow, however, will mercifully omit the usual pedagogy on semantics of purpose, numerology of goals, or techniques of procedure. Instead, those programs will be treated in terms of the agrarian and industrial features of agriculture today.

If modern agriculture is an industrial stem grafted on an agrarian root, so has price and income policy had agrarian and industrial components.

And even as the agrarian and industrial aspects of agriculture are in many respects scarcely compatible, so do they give rise to competition or conflict in design of price and income policies.

HISTORICAL EVOLUTION

The earliest policy in our national history was pure agrarianism. It was to make land available cheap or, best of all, free. From then on, demands from the countryside began to have an air of helping defenseless agrarian farmers wrestle with the growing commercial world. Pressure arose to build roads and railroads ("internal improvements") and to let banks provide lots of money and credit. Later came the Granger movement to break up monopolies that hurt farmers. Grades, standards, and market news were asked for. Meanwhile, research and education came on the scene.

Not until the severe price break of 1920–21 was there a clamor for direct price aid. Leading businessmen who advised the presidents of the 1920s acquiesced only in giving farmers more economic information and making it easier for them to form cooperatives. In 1922 the Bureau of Agricultural Economics began to publish information on the economic outlook, and in the same year the Capper-Volstead Act became law.

The ill-fated Federal Farm Board dated from the late 1920s.

Federal programs for agriculture entered a new historical phase with the enactment of New Deal farm laws during the productive first 100 days of the Roosevelt Administration (1933). Price and income programs adopted since that time have patterned after those first New Deal ones. More than before, the New Deal added industrial features to otherwise agrarian policies.

MODERN POLICIES FOR AN AGRARIAN AGRICULTURE

Farm policies written into law in 1933 might have been almost entirely agrarian except for the devastating industrial depression of the time, which torpedoed demand for all consumer goods including food and clothing. Rather surprisingly, little was done at first to strengthen demand for farm products. The big push was to restore overall employment and income, a strictly industrial approach. It was expected that agriculture would share in regained prosperity.

On the other hand, production and price policies were essentially agrarian. They have largely retained that character.

Agrarian agriculture is nature-bound. It is subject to all the risk and inconstancy that are nature's mark. One year's crops may be huge. The next year's may be devastated by drought. In every year there are seasonal fluctuations in supply and therefore in price, some regular and some erratic.

Some of the techniques of industrial agriculture reduce the risks implicit in nature. Irrigation protects against drought. Chemical pesticides lessen damage from insect plagues. Nevertheless, nature still exercises her sway. Policy actions serve more to mitigate nature's harshness than to prevent it.

Policies have been adopted to even out the financial losses from crop failure, to store harvests from season to season and from year to year, and to adjust production by influencing acreage planted to a crop (usually reducing it). These are the principal agrarian components of U.S. farm policy.

Crop Insurance

An all-risk federal crop insurance program began for wheat in 1938. Programs have been expanded steadily since. In a sense they culminated in the disaster payment provisions of the Agriculture and Consumer Protection Act of 1973. Disaster payments did not displace crop insurance, however.

Crop insurance programs are funded primarily by premiums charged. In the 1973 law, by contrast, any eligible farmer who loses a crop could get a payment on it to the extent of his allotment. The payment was a subsidy from the U.S. Treasury. Disaster payments were an issue of contention in writing a 1977 farm law.

Crop Storage

Storage of crops has been a part of all programs from the 1930s to the 1970s. It has been tied closely to price support; seldom has it had independent status. Originally, price support loans were intended to finance a farmer's holding his crop past the seasonally low prices of harvesttime and to establish a minimum price received. Only after the program had been in operation for several years was it given a third role, that of a food reserve. The Agricultural Adjustment Act of 1938 went farther than any previous one to specify crop-storage objectives.

The 1938 farm law (still partly in force) provided for acquiring stocks of grain and cotton in a year of big crops or weak demand, followed by release in a year of small crops or exceptionally strong demand. This was the ever-normal granary, or the Joseph plan. Thus was nature's alternating niggardliness and generosity to be compensated by man's clever management.

Production Control

It is a moot question whether agrarian philosophies would call for, or even tolerate, programs to restrict production. As a rule the agrarian tradition has eulogized bountifulness. Furthermore, the economic purpose of production control has had a big ingredient of protecting capital values in agriculture. This does not have much agrarian ring to it.

On the other hand, it is clear enough that insofar as production control has been practiced the technique has almost always been agrarian. It has been to adjust cropped acreages up or down. This has been done by acreage allotments, by various general land retirement programs such as the Soil Bank, by rules governing holding acreage in conserving crops, and by more specific programs for idling land such as the set-asides of recent farm law.

Agrarian Market Demand
In the image of an agrarian agriculture, farm products are sold to consumers, that is, to family members who buy food for their tables. Although the existence of middlemen is acknowledged, they are seen as intermediaries whose main role in life is to overcharge for their nominal services.

In the early years of the New Deal farm programs, as explained above, consumer demand was taken into account through general economic policy to restore employment and increase national income. About the middle of that decade attention began to be given to demand for food and farm products. Section 32 of the Act of August 24, 1935, diverted sizable tariff revenues to boosting the market for farm products. Supplementary food programs began more by accident than design, but grew to prominence rather fast.

If enabling family consumers to buy more food is agrarian, the agrarian component of policy had attained high standing by the mid-1970s. At that time the cost of food stamp, school lunch, and minor food programs exceeded $7 billion annually.

POLICIES FOR AN INDUSTRIAL AGRICULTURE
U.S. agriculture has moved far toward industrial structure. Even though high costs of some industrial inputs, notably energy, may be halting the trend or even reversing it slightly, by any measure our agriculture is highly industrialized and will remain so.

An industrial agriculture brings into prominence several characteristics that are absent or muted in an agrarian system. Most of these were touched on in Chapter 3 and are repeated here only to aid in discussion of policy.

1. Industrial farming depends critically upon industrial inputs including the financing with which to buy them. Financing often requires commercial credit.

2. Similarly, farm products are typically sold not to consumers but to a market system that is not a passive intermediary but possessed of economic power and geared for market development. Furthermore, it calls for highly regular and systematic delivery of farm products—what the Germans call rationalization.

3. Industrialization brings its own kind of instability to agriculture.

It is an instability akin to the industrial business cycle. Glenn Johnson's explanation is that fixed assets lead to cycles in production and price of farm commodities. This means that as agriculture uses more industrial inputs with their freewheeling productivity and enters into more industrial-type investment, it becomes prey to cycles in investment and production. The pattern is most prominent in highly industrialized enterprises such as broilers and commercial feeding of cattle.

A fourth point might be made. If agrarian agriculture is nature-bound, industrial agriculture is man-bound. It is a product of human ingenuity.

The difference affects attitudes. Human beings are properly deferential to the powers of the Deity over agrarian agriculture. They can be scornful of how (other) human beings manage industrial agriculture.

That is to say, the psychological setting of an industrial agriculture leads to much more specific aspirations in farm policy—and more resentment if they are not realized. Farmers who are supine before forces of nature can be stirred to activism over the way other people treat them. Consumers who may be fatalistic about how sunshine colors an apple can get excited about market firms that insist on breeding tough-skinned fruit or coating it with a shiny compound. Not agrarian agriculture but an industrial one leads to the sensitivities and agitations known as consumerism.

In the same vein, choice as to internal structure of agriculture is now seen as subject to human decision. We can collectively decide whether we are to have a family farm system, or big corporations, or cooperative farming, or contractual integration, or some other kind of agriculture.

Industrial Element in Stabilization Policies
Depending on industrial prosperity to improve domestic demand for farm products classifies as an industrial contribution to farm policy.

Industrial features show up elsewhere. Methods of production control geared to acreage are agrarian. Those directed to output or non-farm inputs are industrial. In the program for some types of tobacco a farmer gets a poundage rather than an acreage allotment. Also, in two or three marketing orders the delivery quota for a producer comes close to being a quantity quota on output. These selected instances resemble the production or sales quotas established by a commercial firm; they are industrial.

In an industrial agriculture the rate of applying industrial inputs such as nitrogen fertilizer and pumped irrigation water has much effect on production. We might therefore suppose that those inputs rather than land would be the means of production control. It has been suggested that if energy becomes very scarce again, energy-embodied materials might be rationed in line with announced goals for agricultural production. These would be industrial-type controls. As of the mid-1970s the national psychology does not favor that kind of action. Our thinking is still agrarian.

Direct Payments to Farmers. In an important if inconspicuous change in income support, policy for U.S. agriculture has been redesigned to fit its increasingly industrial character.

Such is the meaning of the shift from price supports to direct Treasury payments to shore up farmers' incomes. This shift began during the 1960s and continued in the 1970s. Price supports only affect what a farmer gets for his products. Direct payments are a more sophisticated device that rests on a judgment as to national distribution of income.

Operationally, direct payments can avoid (or at least reduce) the incentive for farmers to intensify and increase production—provided the amount of payment is limited. This proviso is essential. It is contained in the 1973 farm law, which makes each farm's allotment a ceiling on eligibility. If this were not so, that is, if a payment program were open-ended, farmers would have fully as much incentive for all-out production in a direct payment as in a price support program.

Policies to Help Agrarian Farming in an Industrial Setting

The industrial element in agriculture today leads not so much to new policies as to recasting older ones with the purpose of aiding the survival of the agrarian farm unit in an increasingly industrial setting.

Some examples will be cited. One is the almost imperceptible but impressive change in content of research and extension programs. Original programs told a farmer when to plant a crop: agrarian advice. Little extension effort is now devoted to such homely help. More relates to how to use chemicals or to budget big capital expenditures or to procure and manage credit or even to figure income tax. These are industrial in nature.

The family farm has been serviced best in marketing. Grading, inspection and saturation with market information help keep the individual farmer from being engulfed by the magnitude and power of the marketing system. Another kind of marketing activity has regulatory punch to it. It holds a tight rein over trade practices of marketing firms. Closest surveillance is in marketing of livestock and poultry. The Packers and Stockyards Administration stands guard to assure that a farmer gets the last promised dollar for accurately weighed hogs. This is not a minor kind of aid.

Another marketing policy is authorization for farmers' cooperatives. Marketing cooperatives are granted some antitrust exemption. Question may be raised as to whether cooperative organizations are agrarian or industrial. Insofar as they enable small farmers to ship cattle together or negotiate for better prices for processing tomatoes, they are probably agrarian. But when they integrate forward and sell products by an advertised brand name, as Ocean Spray cranberries or Land O'Lakes dairy products, they have modeled after the agribusiness adversary. They have adopted industrial techniques.

Closely akin are marketing orders which likewise facilitate group action in marketing, and collective bargaining. Both have agrarian roots but insofar as they contend with the highly organized marketing system, and in fact pattern after industrial techniques, they relate to the industrial portion of modern agriculture.

Last to be named, and equally ambiguous, is the group action by farmers known as "check-off" promotion of farm products. This promotion patterns after industrial marketing, yet is applied to the raw farm product and in this respect is agrarian. Critics say that industrial promotion pays off only for industrial-type products, which can be merchandised by their brand names. If that be true, extending it to the raw products of agriculture is inappropriate and ineffectual.

SUMMARY

Even as U.S. agriculture today holds tightly to its agrarian forms and yet adds an industrial superstructure, so price and income policy has a mixed, ambiguous agrarian and industrial content.

It is difficult to divide policies sharply into agrarian and industrial. In general, agrarian aspects are pointed toward farmers and their wrestling with inconstancy of nature. Agrarian policies give rise to various means of stabilization of supply and price; industrial orientation is poised toward the imperious marketing system that demands so much orderliness in production and marketing and contains the mechanism for influencing demand and price for farm products. The industrial thrust may account for gradual acceptance of direct payments to regulate farmers' incomes and definitely explains the trend toward more sophisticated arrangements in marketing. The most extreme instance of the latter is forward integration by cooperatives.

It is significant that the industrial component of policies to protect farmers' prices and income is still primarily couched in the old tradition of helping to keep the family farm viable. In many respects industrial pressures lead to replacing the family farm, as by vertical integration, not to sustaining it. Policy relating to the structural organization of agriculture is properly the subject for other chapters.

If you had such a [direct payment] program, it is my belief that there would be limitations to it that would become so restrictive that in effect you would not have any program.
—CONGRESSMAN JAMIE L. WHITTEN

8 TEMPTING ATTRACTIONS OF DIRECT DEFICIENCY PAYMENT PROGRAMS

Even in an age when almost all business is done on paper there is exceptional appeal to a computer-punched check issued by the Treasurer of the United States.

On a stiff blue-green counter the sovereign government of the United States of America declares that it will deliver to a named citizen a specified number of dollers.

Since 1933 billions of such checks conveying many billions of dollars have been received by farmers.

Mention of that watershed year reminds that the farm policy revolution that began then had three features. One, it taught once and for all the lesson that the fortunes of men are not entirely in the hands of the Deity but can be shaped by men themselves. That is, farm policy makes a difference. Two, it authorized joint actions by farmers that had previously been scorned or declared illegal. And three, it opened the doors of the U.S. Treasury to U.S. agriculture.

Unless the direction of policy is sharply reversed, the third lesson, the irresistible attraction of Treasury dollars plus the manipulatory nature of their terms, carries a strong clue to farm affairs of the future.

PAYMENT FOR VALUE RECEIVED?
Except for parity payments that had at least a tinge of deficiency-payment about them, during the New Deal period Treasury dollars were paid to farmers for performance on their part. Puritan attitudes were still strong enough to discourage issuing checks just to support farmers'

income. Money went into building terraces and seeding pastures. Loans were made on grain and cotton, some of which was later delivered to the Commodity Credit Corporation. The USDA assumed certain administrative costs of marketing order programs, which presumably brought more orderliness to marketing. Land retirement programs variously employed the carrot and the stick but there was enough of the former to cost the Treasury lots of money.

Expressed Doubts

Despite requirements that farmers do something in order to get checks, skeptics could question whether a Yankee-hard-sell quid pro quo was being bargained. They could allege with considerable validity that many so-called conservation payments only paid a farmer to do things that were in his own interest. As the Soil Bank and other voluntary land idling schemes came into use, sharp rebukes were heard that payment rates were more generous than necessary, and that farmers often "retired" land they had no intention of cultivating. It was said that the government paid for many phantom acres.

Programs of price support and land retirement in the later 1960s and early 1970s were so obviously generous that no one doubted that they paid farmers more than equivalent land rent. Payments were thinly disguised income supplements as well as rent.

For many years nonrecourse storage loans had been relied on to beef up farmers' incomes in preference to nonpuritanical direct supplements to income. Yet to farmers the loan program almost amounted to largess. To consumers the program had a separate value, as a source of food reserve. Year after year the CCC lent farmers more than the market price and then took over products and disposed of them at a loss. What is the difference, in terms of the role of the Treasury, between that clumsy device and simply paying farmers an above-the-market bonus? This needling question sinks deeper as we realize that the CCC was under tremendous pressure not to carry out the second portion of its assigned mission, namely, to put stored grain and cotton back on the market in a short-crop year. Instead it disposed of its stocks noncommercially, at home and especially abroad. (In the 1960s it finally moved stocks into domestic commercial use in connection with an aggressive new land retirement program, and in so doing infuriated farmers.)

It is not just a play on words to say that farmers received income supplement payments indirectly before they did so directly.

THE CASE FOR DIRECT DEFICIENCY PAYMENTS

All the above is not to deny that in a high proportion of the cases farmers who qualified for checks from the U.S. Treasury contributed some kind of performance. But the various schemes often were generous to the point of hiding considerable governmental beneficence—hiding it in deference to lingering Puritan values.

Taking such pains to keep payments hidden amounted to hypocrisy.

For years the leading advocates of making payments directly and overtly to protect farmers' incomes were those idealistic, ivory tower types, the economists. Those impractical dreamers argued that trying to improve farmers' incomes by lifting commodity prices far above their market level only got everyone into trouble. The technique shrank markets due to the higher prices and built up ever bigger stocks in CCC hands.

Interestingly, the economists had their way when cotton spokesmen, previously violently opposed to any weakening in support price for cotton, decided that too many foreign markets were being lost to other suppliers, and too many domestic markets to synthetics. In a nation that supposedly rejects idealism in favor of pragmatic viewpoints, a costly lesson had to be demonstrated before policy could be altered.

Meanwhile, sponsors of direct payments gained an ally. It was the taxpaying, consuming public. Citizens had become aware of the costliness of federal programs for agriculture. They concluded that if tax money had to be spent, it might as well go for direct payments to supplement lower commodity prices. At least direct payments, unlike price supports, do not add to price of food.

Still another factor leading to direct payments was farmers' aversion to the route of tighter controls. Farmers could, after all, get higher prices in the market without putting so much financial burden on the CCC if they would jointly control their production. When Secretary Freeman proposed such a Spartan policy, even the Farm Bureau advised farmers to vote the proposition down, promising, "We'll get you a softer program."

They did. Voluntary land retirement and direct Treasury payments came steadily into more prominence during the 1960s.

THE SIDE ISSUES

Each move toward direct payments nevertheless aroused a school of critics who wagged fingers and shouted in shrill voices about opening up a Pandora's box of new, divisive, and difficult issues.

They were correct. An overt policy of direct payments was begun and the issues came into view. They would have been more contentious by the mid-1970s were it not for the dormancy in active farm programs. Booming export markets for grain and Administration opposition combined to keep the 1973 farm law essentially inactive in 1973–76. Policy debates became quieter. They also turned more ideological. When nothing practical is immediately involved, ideology can be indulged in conveniently.

For all their attractiveness direct payments open up a boxful of contentious issues that trace primarily to their being so personal, so flexibly adaptable, and so visible.

A Treasury check issued as a loan on a crib of corn is payment *for* a commodity. One of the same size paid under disaster or income-deficiency provisions of a farm law is a payment *to* a farmer. Questions of propriety and eligibility quickly surface, especially as the whole shootin' match comes into public view. For example, scarcely had payments been incorporated into farm programs when word of the size of some checks leaked out. Thereupon an aroused public asked why a California bank should get $4 million for not growing crops, and Senator Eastland a quarter million. The same public, via the legislative process, quickly moved to put a limit on size of individual payments. It was first $55,000 on an individual crop, then $20,000 total, irrespective of the number of crops. A higher figure was sought in 1977.

Prescribed Conditions and Income Distribution

Restated, direct Treasury payments as a program device inevitably introduce issues of what if anything shall be required of a farmer as condition for eligibility and how the payments affect the relative incomes of various categories of farmers.

Once the federal Treasury is tapped, it becomes scarcely resistible to use payments for various purposes including rebalancing income distribution among farmers.

This inevitable outcome may as well be admitted. In any future decline in farmers' prices and incomes the Government will not pay out $3–6 billion without concern for whether the public is getting its money's worth. "Money's worth" could involve whatever goals U.S. citizens have in mind for agriculture. (Getting their money's worth may mean consumers will want price supports and storage rather than such large deficiency payments. See Chapter 12.)

Those goals will almost certainly include some notion of fairness of distribution according to size of farm. The quick action to put a fixed limit on size of payment, referred to above, testifies to public touchiness. The single inflexible limit is a crude way to influence the relative treatment of small and large farmers in a payment program. Some formula for scaling the payment rates would be much sounder. In it the smaller farms, or those that qualify by other criteria, would have their payments scaled upward. The largest farms or those otherwise frowned on would be subject to downward scaling.

Among conditions that might have to be met for a farmer to be eligible for payments, or to get payments at the full rate, are conserving use of land and a preferred tenure arrangement such as owner-operatorship. These will be discussed below. For now, the point to be made is that insofar as direct payments are employed as an instrument of farm policy (as contrasted, for example, with price support loans), the general public will have a voice in setting farm policy. In the language of Chapter 5, payment methods are not neutral with respect to who makes farm policy. The more direct payments are relied on, the less will farmers alone make policy. And when nonfarmers take a hand in making policy involving direct Treasury payments they will ask about prescribed conditions and income distribution.

Direct Payments, Historical Allotments, and Conservation*

It is standard economic lore that direct payments to supplement farmers' income cannot be open-ended lest they break the Treasury. The exception, of course, occurs when increased production is sought, although in that case it is more economical and probably more effective to confine payments to the additional production obtained. This was done for some products in World War II. But putting that exception aside, we run into the simple proposition that if direct payments are generous, they stimulate production and quickly grow to excessive size. Almost all direct payment programs confine the amount of payment to a farmer to a figure proportional to his base allotment.

Most allotments have been historical. Although county committees of the Agricultural Stabilization and Conservation Service have considerable latitude to adjust allotments, in practice they have beeen reluctant to depart far from a farm's history.

The practice makes payment eligibility an accident of history. It tends to keep agriculture static, to work against dynamic change. It favors the older, established farmers over younger ones.

Also, the time-honored practice prevents using the payments to achieve other goals. One such goal is to farm land in a conserving manner. If accident of history is not a sound base for allocating payment money and if it works against the interests of newer farmers, should a conservation goal replace it?

It would be possible to introduce soil conservation as a criterion for a program. Land in farms could be scored according to categories of conserving uses. Eligibility for payments would then depend on a farmer's complying with a conservation plan for his farm. If set-asides (land retirement) were in force, a farmer would of course have to comply with the terms in order to be eligible for payments; but the terms would themselves be calculated from conserving rather than historical bases.

Direct Payments and Structure of Agriculture

Much is said these days about the kind of agriculture we prefer in our country—"kind" in the sense of organizational structure, or who will control it.

---

* Ideas that follow are largely taken from Harold F. Breimyer, *A Farm, Food, and Land-Use Policy for the Future*, statement of the Agriculture Committee, National Planning Association, Washington, D.C., January 1976.

In some respects tenure arrangements were taken into consideration from the beginning of New Deal farm programs. Program rules have related mainly to how payments are to be divided between tenant and landlord. In addition, for a number of years the smallest farms were given concessions in allotments and payment rates. A vestige of that feature was retained in the cotton portion of the 1973 farm law.

Successive farm laws have been enacted in an aura of eloquent dedication to the principle of preserving family farm agriculture. The language has been little more than gesture. Economists suspect that the various price support and direct payment programs have helped large farms more than medium-sized and smaller ones. If that be true, the programs have had effects opposite to the declared purpose.

The limit imposed on size of an individual payment ostensibly favors middle-sized farms against the largest ones. To some degree it may in fact do so. Yet the limit is ambiguous. Under the 1973 law farms subject to it were excused from carrying out the terms of idling land ("set-aside"). So what net effect did that limit have? In some circumstance it might give an advantage to the big farms.

Obviously, the limit does not affect the competitive relationship of farms of various types and sizes that fall below it.

All of which is to say only that, to date, direct Treasury payments have not been designed to influence the structural organization of agriculture to any significant degree.

United States citizens have at least a sentimental preference for retaining a family farm agriculture in our nation. By design or by default the terms of payment programs affect the kind of agriculture we are to have. In any reactivated payment programs, their bearing on who will control agriculture will not escape scrutiny. They will probably be seen and judged accordingly.

Access to the vaults of the U.S. Treasury casts farm programs into more dimensions than were seen when the CCC merely lent farmers money on the corn or cotton they put under seal. Direct payments to remedy a deficiency in farmers' income fit the industrial traits of agriculture, and they bring the general public into an active critique of farm programs.

It is ironic that family farmers have provided much of the voting strength for the continuation of . . . policies that discriminate against them. —PHILIP M. RAUP

9 FARMING'S NONINSTINCT FOR SELF-PRESERVATION

Most species of the animal kingdom have some instinctive capacity that serves to perpetuate their kind. The honey bee is known for organized defense of the colony. The herding instinct among quadrupeds is protective.

Human beings rely on cognition. They consciously, not instinctively, set up social institutions to serve their various purposes. Do they endow their handiwork with capacity for survival?

The historical evidence is that they do badly. Their institutions seem to have a life cycle. Maturity is followed by decline and death. Whole nations trace the pattern.

The family farm is a social institution. It is of human origin. It fits agrarian agriculture and may have originated in response to some of the features of that kind of agriculture. It is less well suited to an industrial agriculture. Therefore the question of whether the family farm is to be retained in a more industrial setting is a policy question.

The thesis to be advanced here is that unless family farmers change their ways of looking at their own nature and their destiny they will fade from the scene. They will become extinct.

Oh, brave shouts of defiance can be heard. Declarations of "nothing is happening" or the irrelevant "the family farm can outcompete" fill the farm policy air. They are but sounding brass. Not the decibel level of affirmation but the wisdom of policy is the key to the kind of agriculture we will have in the future.

The thesis, restated, is that family farming has no instinct for self-preservation.

Until recently little attention was paid to structural organization of agriculture, except for reasking old questions about owner-operatorship versus tenancy. Otherwise, threats to family farming were seen as gossamer. Lately the topic has had more exposure. It has been expanded into the several choices among kinds of agriculture such as contractual, large-corporation, or even a new kind of cooperation. News media, even network TV, give the debates publicity. Some farm organizations show concern.

In the early 1970s extension economists of North Central States generated nationwide discussions on "Who Will Control U.S. Agriculture?" (1) However, states where agriculture had already drifted into big hands found the issue too hot to handle educationally.

WHERE WE NOW STAND

Of all the defensive jargon poured into the air the least correct line is that little is happening and that even now "there ain't nobody here but us little family farmers."

In reality many kinds of farmers are on the scene. The single most pregnant statement to be made is that U.S. agriculture is a medley, a jig-saw mixture of every kind of farming system under the sun. This point was made with some emphasis in Chapter 5.

Categories of farms may be set forth as the following:
1. Smaller than family size
2. Family size, open market
    a. Primarily owner-operated
    b. Primarily tenant-operated
3. Larger than family size, open market
4. Cooperative
5. Contractually integrated
6. Large corporate

The smallest farms (category 1) are usually part-time or retirement farms.

Category 2a is the traditional family farm. It is of family size (usually of not more than 1½ or 2 family workers, with not more than the same number of hired workers). It buys and sells in the market. It is a self-managed proprietorship. Although full owner-operatorship is not required, tenancy cannot be extremely high.

Tenant-operated farms of family size are category 2b.

The third category is of farms larger than family size but owned and operated by farmers and not by nonfarm people or firms.

A cooperative farm is more an economist's category than a prevailing type of farm. Cooperative hog farrowing establishments approximate it. The distinguishing feature of a cooperative farm is that members are bound together by full-contract commitments for joint procurement of inputs and marketing of products.

Contractual integration is familiar. It dominates broilers, for instance. In it, management is transferred to the integrator.

Corporate farming (category 6) refers to total control by industrial-type corporations.

Relative Importance of Farming Systems

Of the categories of farming systems named above, smaller-than-family sized farms and cooperative farms are least important. Although the smallest farms probably number a million, they contribute only a few percent of total marketings of farm products. Cooperative farms are rare. They are, however, a realistic possibility for the future.

Contractual integration has become sizeable for some commodities. Although the Economic Research Service reported that 17 percent of all farm marketings in 1970 came from production contracts (2), a more realistic figure may be about 15 percent. The ERS report counts as integrated various cooperative arrangements in milk marketing that are at best borderline integration. Any estimates of this nature are subject to definitional problems.

Because the Census Bureau still counts all feeding of cattle and production of eggs as within agriculture, thus keeping giant commercial feedlots and egg cities in the statistical fold, industrial-corporation farming ranks as substantial. The Economic Reasearch Service has separately estimated that owner-integrated firms marketed 5 percent of all crops and livestock in 1970, and that large multiestablishment firms accounted for 7 percent of all farm marketings in 1969. Certainly more than 10 percent of all farm output must be credited to large industrial-style corporations.

The rest of U.S. farming is in the hands of family and larger-than-family farmers. How to divide between the two is anyone's guess. It is clear, though, that the larger units are gaining at the expense of family sized ones. In 1969, 75 percent of all the farm product marketings in California came from farms selling $100,000 of products in the year. The figure for Arizona was 86 percent, for Florida 73 percent, for Texas 46 percent. Even for Nebraska it was 40 percent. The greater threat to family farming, at least in the shorter run, may come not from outside agriculture but from within it.

THE NUB OF FAMILY FARMING'S VULNERABILITY

Another proverb about family farming needs to be speared. It is that family farming will survive because it is more efficient than any other kind of farming. This is false.

Not the premise but the conclusion is false. With a few exceptions such as commercial livestock feeding, family farming does indeed compare favorably in efficiency. The peculiar features of agriculture deny any material advantage to large size.

But operating efficiency is not the controlling factor. The contest is being waged on other grounds. Those grounds involve what is sometimes called the intangibles in agriculture. They have to do with advantages in buying supplies, and getting credit, and marketing product. Large corporate establishments simply are able to negotiate better delivery terms and tap cheaper credit sources than family farmers can. They especially can do so when their only competitors are family farmers. They may even generate a little market power in their procurement and marketing, at the expense of family farmers.

These intangibles have to do also with tax advantages. Deductions from income taxes have become an immense subsidy to U.S. agriculture. The economics of farm management these days is just as much a matter of manipulating tax rules as of choosing fertilizers and balancing rations.

Still other intangibles come into being via the many kinds of environmental and other regulations now being imposed on agriculture. A running fight with the Environmental Protection Agency has centered on whether rules to control feedlot pollution would be so drawn as to give the commercial lot a better break than farmer feeders. After several false starts that brought alarm, EPA rules announced in 1976 were relatively considerate of modest sized livestock and poultry operations.

It is precisely because the family farm's only relative advantage lies in the "tangible" of operating efficiency and does not extend to intangibles that its survival is in jeopardy.

The Family Farmer's Self-image
The problem of the family farmer's survival begins with his own self-image. At the drop of a hint the farmer will recount all the heroic independence and self-reliance he displays and what virtues they are in our flimsy, character-less society. These qualities are not to be decried. They are splendid. They are particularly well suited to the agrarian portion of agriculture.

Those qualities omit group consciousness. They have no social content—no schooling for joint action. They contribute nothing toward developing a sense of what is required not for a farmer but for *farmers* to survive in an increasingly industrial agriculture.

Group consciousness refers to the relationship of the individual farmer to the many joint and public aspects of farming. It normally leads to accepting the group discipline that goes with that relationship.

But above all else group consciousness involves a capacity to perceive differences between how the various intangibles—laws and rules and marketing arrangements and such—affect the farmer as an individual versus the farmer as a part of a group.

Often the individual farmer, lacking group consciousness, judges and responds to laws and rules only according to how they relate to him directly. He can be oblivious to how they affect him indirectly via consequences upon all his fellow farmers.

Theoretical economists express the same difference in the Latin words of micro versus macro consequences. Most farmers see only the micro. Their failure to see joint (macro) consequences may cost them common survival.

University professors try to teach the same idea to their students in the language of "fallacy of composition." McConnell says in a standard text, "This fallacy contends that 'what is true for the individual or part is necessarily also true for the group or whole.' This is a logical fallacy; it is not correct." He explains that what is true for the individual need not be true "for the group or whole" (3).

Students dutifully recite the definition back to the professor. They show little capacity to apply it.

Special Advantage of the Large Corporation

A word more may illustrate and clarify. Many family farmers believe their principal adversary to be the large industrial corporation as epitomized in the farming activities of the Tenneco conglomerate. They could be correct. But in comparing their resources with Tenneco's, to their own reassurance, they fail to appreciate a special capacity of the large corporation. It is to arrive at and autocratically impose a single corporate position for commercial dealings and political maneuver. In the corporation internal strictures and debates are reconciled and resolved—and kept hidden from the outside world. The big corporation is monolithic and it acts accordingly. It is an entity. In today's world that is an attribute of major importance.

FARMING'S DIVISIVENESS

A number of examples could be offered about farming's penchant to divide so as to be conquered. Only a few will be named here. They begin with divisions of interest in foreign trade.

Foreign Trade

Agriculture is a big net exporter. Any trade restrictionism hurts it as a whole and is likely to hurt every part of it including import commodities. Beef is now imported. Inshipments of dry Australian cow beef have become a policy symbol exceeding their importance to anyone. The quota limiting the quantity imported adds little to the price of the Good and Choice steers that are the main product of our industry. It is market shrinking as it encourages development and use of fabricated soybean substitutes. A weightier effect is that the quota, like all nontariff barriers to trade, induces retaliation against our farm exports.

So long as the United States is quick to protect its own food imports it deals from a weak hand when it tries to talk Common Market countries, for example, into liberalizing their restrictions against our farm exports. Yet each threat of new imports of beef or palm oil or any other product raises new farm hackles.

Pollution Control

Given reasonable enviromental regulations, family feeders of cattle or hogs can probably control pollution more readily than large feedlots can. They can also recycle wastes. It therefore is ironic when family farmers come to the defense of feedlots that protest the regulations imposed on them. Farmer feeders might be better off if big feedlots were tightly regulated.

Land Use Controls

To repeat a theme developed in a previous chapter, although many farmers resist all kinds of land use controls their future may depend on them. It is entirely possible that within 50 or 75 miles of metropolitan areas family farming can survive in the long run only under the aegis of land use rules that, while possibly repugnant to some individual farmers, offer farming an essential protection.

Income Tax Rules

It is in the tax area* that we have the clearest instance where farmers ask for and get concessions that help them individually and kill them collectively.

This particularly applies to medium-sized farmers who are not usually in high tax brackets. Any income tax concession puts them at a competitive disadvantage relative to wealthier taxpayers receiving the same concession.

Principal provisions of tax law that affect farmers in this way are the cash basis option in paying taxes, the deductible investment rule that permits certain expenditures of investment nature to be deducted currently instead of depreciated, and the lower tax rates on capital gains. Most powerful of all is a combination of deductible investment and capital gains. Money put into some kinds of orcharding can be deducted

---

* For a reliable source of information on this subject see *How Federal Income Tax Rules Affect Ownership and Control of Farming,* North Central Regional Extension Publication 37, University of Illinois at Urbana-Champaign, Cooperative Extension Service Special Publication 32, 1974; and *Income Tax Rules and Agriculture,* University of Missouri-Columbia, Agricultural Experiment Station Special Report 172, 1975. The Tax Reform Act of 1976 invalidated only a little of the information contained in the reports.

from current income tax liability. An equivalent amount of the eventual return from the operation can then be reclassified into capital gain. Capital gain incurs tax at scarcely half the rate paid on ordinary income.

An example will illustrate. To keep it simple, transactions are assumed to take place quickly enough that there is no depreciation or interest charge. An investor puts $10,000 into an operation and sells out for $15,000. Assume first that the money put in counts as deductible investment. The $15,000 received then classifies entirely as capital gain. If the investor is in the 60 percent tax bracket he saved $6,000 as a tax deduction from other income when he made his investment. His tax on half the capital gain is $4,500. He saves $1,500 on taxes and gets $5,000 profit on the operation, for a total after-tax profit of $6,500. If the investor were in the 20 percent tax bracket he would have had only a $2,000 tax deduction and would have paid $1,500 tax on profit. His after-tax net is less than the richer investor's—$5,500.

Next make the operation depreciable. The capital gain is reduced to $5,000. There is no tax deduction. The 60 percent investor pays $1,500 capital gains tax and has an after-tax profit of $3,500. The 20 percent taxpayer pays $500 tax and gets an after-tax profit of $4,500. The data summarize:

	Overall Profit	
Investment rule	*60% tax bracket*	*20% tax bracket*
Deductible	$6,500	$5,500
Depreciable	3,500	4,500

When combined with capital gains tax rates, the deductible investment privilege gives three times as great a bonus compared with depreciable investment to the investor who is in the 60 percent tax bracket as to the 20 percent one.

Equally significant is that deductible investment, in this illustration, makes the after-tax income greater than the actual operating profit. It is $1,500 greater for the high tax person, and $500 for the low tax one.

This last observation leads to the first of two principal objections raised about tax-subsidy financing of agriculture. It is that such tax rules help the high income investor much more than one of more modest income. The difference is so wide that investors using a farming operation as tax shelter can make money on their maneuver even though the operation itself runs a loss. Self-financing farmers cannot compete with tax-subsidized operations.

In the Midwest the most heralded instance of this kind of competition is the cattle feeding businesses in areas such as the High Plains of Texas that were set up as limited partnerships. Farmer feeders of Missouri cannot stand up against feedlot competition financed by tax write-offs.

Granted, when the bottom fell out of cattle feeding in 1974 even the tax shelter investors lost money. They quickly lost heart too. A number of feedlots went through the financial wringer. But the operations sprang up again later.

The cattle feeding experience illustrates the second objection to tax sheltered financing of farming. It is that funds induced by such attractions lead to episodes of overexpansion, and to cyclical boom and bust. Anticipating just that outcome, citrus and almond producers some years earlier had asked Congress to cancel the deductible investment privileges previously granted them. Those producers, more discerning than most farmers, saw tax-subsidized investment as too unstabilizing.

Estate Tax Rules

At the time of writing this essay farm circles were agog with campaigns to reduce federal tax rates on farm estates. Some demands were to liberalize estate taxes selectively (i.e., for farm estates only), others to do so generally. The most popular proposal was to increase the amount of exemption, which had long been $60,000. Although no summary judgment will be offered here, the arguments advanced were a perfect illustration of absence of group consciousness. They were a pure case of fallacy of composition.

A higher estate tax exemption would indeed help keep a farmer's farm in *his* family, as advocates claimed. However, some surveys show that in only a fourth of all instances does a farm remain with heirs. Further, not all heirs want to stay on the farm and farm it.

It is an entirely different matter whether the family farm as an institution would be strengthened.

In general, the same rule applies to estate taxes as to income taxes: the more liberal the concessions, the more will wealthy persons be benefited relative to those of modest means, including wealthy nonfarmers relative to ordinary farmers.

Bigger estate tax exemptions would make farm investments more attractive to high income nonfarmers. They would also favor established farmers who have accumulated sizable estates. The larger the exemptions, the more will land holding within agriculture drift into a hereditary pattern. To make farm ownership essentially hereditary would be opposite to what has been declared as the American tradition.

Or to counter more brusquely the argument made by proponents of estate tax liberalization, selling off parcels of farm estates in order to pay taxes is not a priori objectionable. On the contrary, it is exactly what is needed in order to keep the door of opportunity open to new farmers.

Reversing the line of argument once more, one of the best ways to strengthen and protect family farming as such—if that goal be sought—is to keep estate taxes sharply graduated. They would restrain the trend toward larger-than-family farms, whether nonfarmer- or farmer-owned.

Family farmers who really want to protect family farming should beg for graduated estate taxes.

And to echo the idea of paradox in farm affairs, as a general rule it will be easier to keep farming in the hands of actual farmers if taxes on return to investment are kept higher rather than lower. For family farming to survive, the positive to be accentuated is not return to landholding, but return to land-farming.

THE TRAGEDY OF THE COMMONS

Farmers like other human beings seek individual satisfactions, but as they do not live alone on Robinson Crusoe's island they can realize those satisfactions only in a group or social context.

By virtue of their agrarian tradition family farmers are unusually conscious of their individual roles and performance. They are equally unschooled regarding necessary terms of interaction with their fellows.

This has been the theme developed thus far in this essay.

As agriculture becomes more industrial traditional patterns of thinking and of action become outmoded. Terms of relationship with the rest of the economy take control. Underdeveloped group consciousness looms as an obstacle, even, perhaps, a fatal one.

An entirely different way to view the same picture is as the tragedy of the commons.

James Horsfall poses the situation in these words:

As you may remember, in medieval Britain and colonial United States, every village had a commons. The most famous in this country, of course, was the Boston Commons. All New England villages had these, although they were generally called the village green rather than the commons. In those days, of course, almost everyone had to have a cow because there were no dairies; hence the villages created the commons as a place to pasture cows. Everyone had a right to pasture a cow on the commons. This system worked fine as long as the village was small and the commons was big enough to support the cattle.(4)

Horsfall then points out that the villagers had infinite freedom. They had it so long as their cow herd stayed below the capacity of the commons, which was finite. When too many new villagers arrived and too many cows were pastured, the commons was put under stress.

Updating the parable, we all can enjoy our commons in its various forms so long as demands on it do not exceed its capacity. The analogy applies many places—to capacity of highways to take automobiles, of parks to shelter people, of air to diffuse pollution, and of water to absorb wastes.

Agricultural resources are a kind of commons. Many are already under stress. Rules have been developed in some cases to reduce that stress. Grazing districts restrict herd count lest the grass be damaged. Drainage districts regulate water flow. Environmental regulations in farming fit the same analogy: application of chemicals on soil is kept within the soil's capacity to assimilate them.

One of the best analogies to putting too many cows on the commons is sinking too many wells into underground water. In various places in our Plains aquifers are being pumped for irrigation faster than the water can recharge. The inevitable outcome will be not merely to put that commons under stress, but to destroy it.

Awareness of pressure on our agricultural commons is a group consciousness appropriate to our era.

WHAT DOES IT MATTER?

This essay has ranged far and wide, elaborating farming's noninstinct for self-preservation into philosophical reflections.

In an agrarian agriculture the family farm was relatively secure. In a more industrial agriculture it is relatively insecure. Whether it is to be adapted so as to be worth preserving, and how that might be brought about, are policy questions.

Is the game worth the candle?

The question stirs debates. The criteria for a judgment are not merely economic. They are social too—they reach to our basic values.

The majority of farmers and of the general public will always declare in an opinion poll that they favor the family farm. Among skeptics or opponents are some, though not all, agribusinessmen, and some, though not all, ivory tower scholars.

Apparently family farmers like their role. They resist shifting to contractual or wage status. Rural communities are generally profamily farm because so much of both their economic and social structure is based on it.

The general public? Apparently the mundane and the idealistic combine to form the public judgment. Citizens are dreadfully fearful of monopolization in food production. A nation that will tolerate powerful oligopolies in business machines and pharmaceuticals is adamant against letting the Tennecos take over agriculture and the pricing of food.

At the other extreme there remains a vestigal identification with the spiritual attributes associated with the family farm. Whitney Griswold put it well years ago: "The family farm . . . is the daydream of city-dwellers. . . . For millions of Americans it represents a better world, past but not quite lost, one to which they may still look for individual happiness or, maybe, national salvation" (5).

The basic issues in a family farm agriculture are not those of productivity. Family farming is neither clearly inferior nor clearly superior in productiveness to other farming systems. The fundamental issues are of other nature. Farming is now the one remaining large industry that has resisted the giant conglomerate form of business, now pushing its octopus arms to much of the economy. Without protective action farming will not remain untouched. If there is any public wish to restrain the conglomerate business system, farming could be the Rubicon past which it is not allowed to go.

The second issue springs out of farming's peculiar agrarian base of the land. Land is essential and it is intrinsically scarce. In a growing nation its scarcity and differential productiveness yield an ever increasing unearned income, in the form of rent and capital gain. These have the capacity to underreward labor and management, and to break agriculture into sharply differentiated social and economic classes. The magic virtue of family farming is that these incomes become integrated with return to land as a seat of employment. They are part of a composite return to those multirole persons who do the work, provide the management, and assume the risk. They are not divisive.

Farming's noninstinct for self-preservation? It is innocent in an agrarian agriculture where survival depends on individual performance. It is perilous in a more industrial agriculture. In an agriculture that is more industrial than agrarian, survival may depend on group consciousness and on understanding that what looks good to farmers individually may doom them collectively.

NOTES

1. *Who Will Control U.S. Agriculture?* North Central Regional Extension Publication 32, College of Agriculture, Special Publication 27, (Urbana-Champaign: Univ. of Ill. 1972). *Who will Control U.S. Agriculture?* North Central Regional Extension Publication 32–1 through 32–6, College of Agriculture, Special Publication 28, (Urbana-Champaign: Univ. of Ill. 1973). *How Federal Income Tax Rules Affect Ownership and Control of Farming,* North Central Regional Extension Publication 37, College of Agriculture, Special Publication 32, (Urbana-Champaign: Univ. of Ill. 1974). *Death and Taxes: Policy Issues Affecting Farm Property Transfers,* North Central Regional Extension Publication 40, College of Agriculture, Special Publication 38, (Urbana-Champaign: Univ. of Ill. 1975).
2. Ronald L. Mighell and William S. Hoofnagle, *Contract Production and Vertical Integration in Farming, 1960 and 1970,* U.S. Dept. of Agr., Econ. Res. Serv., ERS–479, 1972.

3. Campbell R. McConnell, *Economics: Principles, Problems, and Policies,* 2nd ed. (New York: McGraw-Hill, 1963), p. 15.
4. James G. Horsfall, "Agricultural Strategy in the Tragedy of the Commons," *Agricultural Science Review,* U.S. Dept. of Agr., first quarter 1972, p. 19.
5. A. Whitney Griswold, *Farming and Democracy* (New York: Harcourt, Brace, 1948), p. 5.

Marketing is part and parcel of the modern productive process, the part at the end that gives point and purpose to all that has gone before. —O. V. WELLS

10 FARMERS AND THEIR MARKETS

In the essays presented until now the focus has been on farmers and their relation to land. Only twice was the place of markets mentioned. A (partially) industrial agriculture was shown to require good input and product markets. The definition of a family farm prescribed open market access.

The kind of markets available goes far to characterize the kind of agriculture that will prevail.

The traditional market system has been on a decline for a long while. Its fading has been gradual, and although the easing out has not gone unnoticed it has largely gone undefended. The nature of the decline and the problems it poses are the subject of this chapter.

HISTORICAL GENESIS OF OPEN MARKETS

Development of a system of markets is one of the exciting stories of U.S. agriculture. Rudiments of a system were inherited from Europe and particularly from England. There, as farming improved and the rigid restrictions of the feudal estate were eased, surplus farm products were brought to newly formed town markets, called fairs. The peasant sold his cabbages or his goose, and with the money received he bought household items from the artisans that had established themselves near-by. The markets were protected by the king. They were also made subject to rules, such as those prohibiting practices known by the quaint Old English words forestalling, regrating, and engrossing.

Those early markets performed at one and the same time two functions that still are integral to marketing: they delivered product and they established value.

To establish value through open trading was revolutionary. Throughout the Middle Ages value was pretty much decreed. Churchmen advanced the doctrine of a just price. Those practices anticipated the "administered prices" that big industrial firms establish today, and that today as then can arouse suspicion about their fairness.

When it was seen that price could be established in an open market, that institution was acclaimed. It had the obvious virtues of being impersonal and of protecting the integrity of each party to the transaction. Neither became subordinate to the other.

Markets for farm products became prototype for a market system. The whole idea was incorporated in the doctrines of Adam Smith and other radical thinkers, whom we now call conservative classicists. It is worth noting that the English model imposed stern terms. Medieval rules against forestalling, rebating, and engrossing were extended in the emerging market system to require that there be many traders. In that way no one could wield market power. Though obeisance is still paid, the exacting requisites of a system of self-regulating markets have somehow become lost in the economic system of our time.

Versions of the medieval fair market for farm products remain with us. Best examples are central markets for livestock and the open markets for fresh produce that are found in many cities.

The Market and the Middleman

The early markets like their replicas today did little except deliver a product and price it. They did not process and they certainly did not promote. When commercial firms first became intermediaries they too did little more than store and deliver. They were known as middlemen, a properly descriptive label. Their supposedly nominal role led to their being castigated. The unfriendliness has not disappeared to this day.

Heirs of those middlemen are more than intermediaries. They do much; they dominate. We therefore switch to a structural account of our markets.

MARKETS AND MARKET STRUCTURE TODAY

The 19th century saga of growing importance of well-organized markets for trading in farm commodities has turned in this century to a story of their decline.

Traditional markets are on the downgrade with respect to establishing value (price). More than that, they are being metamorphosed into an industrially poised market system. The market system in our era does not just take the product reaching it and deliver it. It processes and packages; it manages and promotes; it "develops."

In the process the system aggrandizes. It makes motions toward enveloping farming. Some are false but others are genuine. Best illustration is contractual integration by market firms, now pervasive enough to be classed as one category of farming structure (Chapter 9). But apart from individual firms' integration, in ways both subtle and blunt the marketing system virtually overwhelms farming itself. Once only an intermediary between the farmer and consumer, the marketing system is becoming the king of the food-system jungle.

Statistics help to substantiate the changed relationship. The marketing system now absorbs 60 percent of consumers' expenditures for farm products as valued at retail stores. If we add consumer spending in restaurants, the marketing share rises to two-thirds.

But farmers do not get the rest. They pay out more than half their income for goods and services they buy. Some estimates are that farmers—that is, the farming operation—receive only about 12 percent of what consumers spend for food.

One reminder is necessary, however. Just as agriculture as a whole is poised midway between agrarian and industrial structure, and just as farms and farmers are a mixture of all types, even so is the marketing system heterogeneous. It contains all sorts of pricing and delivery methods, some ancient and some contemporary. In general, livestock and their products follow more traditional paths. Grains including soybeans go into various kinds of manufacturing, costly and highly promotional, that are as modern as spaceships and that absorb most of the price the consumer pays. Various other products lie in between.

Trading among Nonequals
Exchange trading presupposes that the parties to transactions are on equal footing. If one side holds an advantage, the results of trading will prove inequitable.

Even though not uniform, the marketing system from farm to consumer is now generally marked by capacity to exercise power. In some cases the power comes from concentration, in others from market development. Not infrequently, as in breakfast cereals, the two are combined.

Another feature of the marketing system is the tougher demands it is putting upon farmers as to kind of product desired. In the old agrarian model of farming, farmers harvested whatever nature gave them. The consumer in turn accepted it uncomplainingly. In a more industrial agriculture linked to an industrial marketing system, a pressure arises for orderly marketing. It calls for better control of quality, regular delivery—in short for the "rationalization" that is so hard to achieve in biological processes. In some instances marketing firms' integration reflects their desire to exercise quality control directly.

Nor is the market system free of power as it extends to local marketing. In an extension service report Love, Marion, and Padberg declare that many local market situations lack what is necessary for good, sharp competition. "Local markets usually are very concentrated with only one or two buyers in some cases. Buyers are frequently in a superior bargaining position."

Furthermore, "many markets are 'thin,' i.e., prices are based on spot or cash markets but only a small share of the production is sold in cash markets" (1).

All of which is not to say that the marketing system is viciously exploitive of timid defenseless farmers. The message is rather to emphasize how radically the marketing system has changed over the years. It is big and influential. Farmers are pygmies wrestling with a monster. They are like a Finland alongside a Soviet Union, or a Luxembourg wedged between France and Germany.

The marketing system is no longer a passive intermediary between farmer and consumer but possessor of the controlling initiative. Farmers do not now produce consumer-ready foods that the marketing system only conveys. More and more they produce a raw material that the marketing system shapes and trims and perhaps fabricates and labels and promotes. The momentum now is with marketers, not with farmers.

The terms of relationships between farmers and their markets will go far to determine the composition and welfare of the agriculture of the future.

Price-discovery Systems

The old system of assembling products at central points where many buyers and sellers could congregate, haggle over price, exchange title, and in the process estabish a going price is now confined to a small fraction of the marketing of farm products.

Departures take three different forms. One is central selling by description instead of inspection. Commodity exchanges, particularly for grains, are the most familiar example. This method is generally regarded as an improvement over central assembly of product, because it saves the cost of physical handling.

A second is direct trading. It is convenient, but it has the disadvantage that buyers and sellers usually are not in close proximity. Unless a lot is done to get good communication it is hard to achieve sharp, effective competition.

The third departure has already been referred to. It is marketing, or market delivery, under production contract. It is entirely different. It is even debatable whether delivery under production contract, like all intrafirm transfers, qualifies as marketing (2).

Terms of delivery and compensation under production contract are normally arranged in advance. Although it has been suggested that contracts be standardized and offered for auction trading, nothing like this has been done. Instead, the route taken most often is to enter into collective bargaining (see next chapter).

Other marketing and pricing methods could be named. In eggs and carcass beef, formula pricing is common. Auctions by telephone or telegraph have been tried in some places, particularly for feeder livestock, sometimes with success.

Farming's Noninstinct

We return to the psychology of an agrarian agriculture. It is not well suited to dealing with the problems introduced by the fading of the traditional open market connection to a marketing system that is becoming ever more assertive. Small farmers cannot individually grapple with big marketers. They can resolve their marketing problems only by joining with their fellows to work out satisfactory solutions.

What solutions they decide on will not be the same for all products. Actions may in fact differ widely. One possible route is to devise new methods of arriving at price. A 1976 report of a Senate Agricultural Committee subcommittee outlines a number of possibilities, some of them exciting (3). Improved government services could be sought—even truly effective enforcement of antitrust against food processing oligopolies!

Another governmental route is to rely once more on relatively high commodity price supports. These can be the ultimate protection to farmers, as indeed they once were. Let the marketing system behave as it will: farmers will be protected by a guaranteed support price. It is not mere coincidence that price supports have been used primarily for commodities in which the marketing system dominates and a small share of consumers' spending gets back to the farmer.

Or farmers could decide on more group action in marketing. This promises much but requires much too. It requires attitudes and aptitudes for which agrarian farmers are not prepared. Their noninstinct for group consciousness and therefore for group action impedes them.

Problems That Vanish

Lest this preaching be too solemn, let it be admitted that price cycles interfere with farmers' stick-to-itiveness in wrestling with marketing problems. Without the cycles it would be hard to explain why even agrarian farmers confess their poorer ability to market than to produce, yet refuse to do much about it. During any period of low prices farmers do in fact come to meetings and tell each other they must investigate their system of marketing. About the time their resolve gets lifted to the sticking place and a battery of committees is appointed, prices rebound. With a price gain of a dime or a dollar problems seem to vanish. Interest does too.

Farmers are like the boy in the Mexican song. Why patch the roof that is leaking rain today, when the sun is sure to shine tomorrow? Why worry about marketing today, when prices are certain to go up tomorrow?

"MARKETS" FOR WHAT FARMERS BUY

All that has been said to this point pertains to markets for the products farmers produce. It has not borne on so-called "input markets"—

procurement of the commercial inputs farmers use in such large quantity.

Input supplying industries are in general even more oligopolistic than the processors and retailers of farm products. Terms of farmers' relationships to their suppliers are just as strategic as those with the handlers of their products. In a partially industrial agriculture the old habit of looking only to the right toward product markets, and not to the left toward input markets, is a major failing. And farmers' non-instinct for what they must do together in their own collective interest applies as menacingly to their procurement of supplies as to any other part of the complicated world of modern agriculture.

NOTES

1. Harold G. Love, Bruce W. Marion, and Daniel I. Padberg, "Who Will Control It?" *Your Food: A Food Policy Basebook,* National Public Policy Education Committee Publication Number 5, Cooperative Extension Service (Columbus: Ohio State Univ. November 1975), p. 56.
2. Harold F. Breimyer, *Economics of the Product Markets of Agriculture* (Ames: Iowa State Univ. Press, 1976), p. 7.
3. U.S. Senate, Committee on Agriculture and Forestry, Subcommittee on Agricultural Production, Marketing, and Stabilization of Prices, *Marketing Alternatives for Agriculture: Is There a Better Way?* 94th Cong., 2nd sess., 1976. A set of leaflets bearing the same overall title was published under aegis of the National Public Policy Education Committee, funded by the Extension Service, USDA.

Farm operators are being compelled to reexamine their organizations in light of changes in the economic organization of agriculture, with little time to do so.

—RANDALL E. TORGERSON

11 HESITANCY IN COOPERATIVE ACTION

In any description of modern farming in the United States, generalizations are suspect and conclusions drawn from them scarcely reliable.

So it is regarding farmers' group action. To say that farmers are so proudly independent that they will not join in cooperative endeavor is grossly wrong. Neighborliness has always been a part of the agrarian tradition. Fortunately, it has not entirely disappeared. Some farmers' cooperatives for procurement or marketing get the laurels of being ranked on both *Fortune* magazine's 500 and the Department of Justice's list of firms under antitrust suspicion.

The only generalization is that no generalization is possible. Or if one be essayed the title to this chapter may come closest: U.S. farmers have not rejected group action but have hesitated in moving toward it.

KINDS OF GROUP ACTIVITY

Formally organized group or cooperative action is usually classified about as follows:

1. Supply or marketing cooperatives
2. Marketing agreements and orders
3. Collective bargaining associations
4. Check-off commodity promotion

These four categories omit activities of more limited nature such as cooperative farm management services and dairy herd improvement associations. Nor do they include politically oriented general farm organizations or the newer commodity organizations.

The four are so familiar that it is scarcely necessary to describe them. Farmers' cooperatives are organized under laws of the various states. Those engaged in marketing come under the aegis of the Capper-Volstead Act of 1922 which gives them some antitrust protection. Marketing orders (more significant than agreements) amount to governmentally enforced cooperation. Under them producers of a commodity can establish certain terms of "orderly marketing" if they can get both their fellows and the Secretary of Agriculture to agree. Sometimes they must also win the approval of a majority of their marketing firms. Not all farm products are eligible for marketing orders. The enabling law "exempts" many important ones. U.S. agriculture as a whole is not ready to accept the group discipline that an order can apply.

Regional orders have proved to work better than those organized interregionally or nationally.

Collective bargaining refers to joint negotiation of price and other terms of trade.

Check-off promotion activities, popular now, allow a deduction to be made from what marketing firms pay farmers for their products. The money so collected is used for commodity promotion, broadly defined to include research. Check-off promotion is newer than the other three kinds of group action and somewhat different from them.

Common Characteristics and Problems
Four points can be made about the first three kinds of group action:
   a. All are a departure from the purest kind of traditional agriculture where independent proprietary farms individually buy and sell in the market. All compromise that model in some way and to some degree.
   b. The rationale for group action springs from the nature of the marketing system—its power, and its stress on orderliness. The rationale goes further, and in so doing presents another paradox, this one almost biblical: farmers can retain the essence of their proprietary status only if they give up a part of it. They give it up, of course, to their own group organizations.
   c. Paradoxical or not, a stumbling block to joint action is farmers' own diversity. The question "who are farmers?" is not merely academic.
   d. A fourth point appears to farmers as an outright contradiction. It seems to them that as soon as they show capacity to join together effectively they come under unfriendly scrutiny. Again in biblical analogy, legal rights are given and legal rights are taken away.

Nontraditional Action to Save Traditional Farming
The first two points are familiar enough. The industrial features of farming reduce it to a thin wedge between the big input supplying sector and that of marketing. As noted in Chapter 10, the market system

of open and visible exchange between equals, the connecting link relied on for two or three centuries, is coming under stress. Group action is one alternative to individual farmers' marketing.

Broad categories of group action can be captioned in two earthy aphorisms, "If you can't lick 'em, join 'em," and "If you can't join 'em, lick 'em."

"Join 'em" means embracing marketing firms' own style of operation. It means bringing industrial marketers' techniques to farming. One way is just to convert farming into industrial corporations, as is now happening in cattle feeding and some vegetable-growing in the West. But that eliminates proprietary farming. The other route is to form cooperatives that venture far backward or forward or both. This is cooperative vertical integration. The ultimate would be to extend cooperatives through processing all the way to retailing. This is now done in a few instances.

It is of course not necessary that an industry be converted entirely to cooperatives. The maxim of the yardstick, which says that good cooperatives keep competitors efficient and honest, still contains much truth.

Cooperatives that integrate forward commonly develop their own branded products, just as any private firm does. Land-O'-Lakes dairy products are an example.

For farmers to knit together in aggressive organizations of this kind requires a discipline that has long been resisted. In Chapter 9 a cooperative agriculture was named as a viable kind of agriculture. It was also admitted there that most farmers are not yet prepared to transfer so much managerial prerogative to their cooperative.

Often, cooperatives that integrate forward successfully have had the benefit of an accompanying marketing order. If this route were to be taken generally in U.S. agriculture, either the marketing order authority would have to be extended to more products or the even stronger marketing board would have to be adopted. To date marketing orders have been limited in scope and the marketing board idea rejected.

Ever since the 1920s when Aaron Sapiro stalked the farm country, cooperative processing and distribution has had its advocates. Some of them have been enthusiastic and eloquent. To date the notable successes have been confined to a relatively few commodities. Citrus, cranberries, and some other specialty crops have been most conspicuous. Some dairy and poultry operations have won prominence. But by and large the notion of effective farmers' cooperatives is exhorted more than it is acted on.

Check-off promotion fits the "join 'em" category. However, promotion of farm products is not quite the same as industrial promotion. It involves promoting not a brand-named final product but individual farm products as such. It has grown in use as some farm leaders conclude there is a payoff for promoting beef or soybeans in the way Kellogg hawks corn flakes and Proctor and Gamble its soaps. Most economists are apostates, doubting that product promotion achieves much. But they are as lacking in proof of the negative as promotion advocates are of the positive.

Licking 'Em. The best example of licking 'em is collective bargaining. It came about partly because of failure to form commodity-handling cooperatives big enough to control the market and make the price. Thereupon some farm groups took a different tack. It was to form negotiating organizations large and powerful enough to bargain with handlers or processors. They have been most successful in milk and fruits and vegetables for processing.

A couple of features of the marketing of those commodities help to explain why bargaining has worked. In milk, the marketing order has been an important if not essential companion device. Fruits and vegetables for processing are primarily contract crops, and their processing industries are highly oligopsonistic (and oligopolistic too). Contractual farming lends itself especially well to collective bargaining. Not a few farm leaders believe that if agriculture goes contractual, collective action in writing the terms of contracts is farmers' only hope.

Collective bargaining requires group discipline. This is an impediment.

Who Are Farmers?

A question of identity of farmers arises because cooperative action is attained most easily when there is homogeneity among membership. A Percheron and a pony do not make a good team at harness, and neither do a 6-section wheat farmer and a weekend player-at-farming join well in a cooperative. Part-time farmers, whose own interests and income sources are divided, do not show close fraternal bonds with full-time farmers.

Nevertheless, the crucial issue concerns agribusiness firms that engage in farming. Ought they be considered "farmers" and allowed to join in cooperatives the same as any proprietary family farmer? If they do so, forming combines of giant strength, should the antitrust protection of Capper-Volstead be extended to them?

In 1971 Breimyer and Torgerson, in a modest piece that got wide publicity, suggested that Capper-Volstead was not intended to protect industrial corporation farmers from antitrust. They added that if the law were bent to do so it would itself come into jeopardy (1). Several years later the issue came to a head as the National Broiler Marketing Association sought the protection of Capper-Volstead. Among the Association's members were big firms such as Allied Mills and Cargill. One of the objects of the group was to stabilize the volume of broiler production, and its proposed methods were at least suspect under antitrust law. The Association's defense was that its members were producers of a farm commodity and therefore "farmers."

When the Department of Justice enjoined the Association a court test was brought. A District Court ruled against Justice and in favor of the Association. In 1977 the Circuit Court reversed the District Court's ruling.

A similar case involving labor law also arose in the poultry industry. An integrated poultry producer said that because it was a farmer it was exempt from the terms of federal labor law. In this instance a state court decided with the company and against the government but the Circuit Court reversed the decision. The case then went to the U.S. Supreme Court, which declared the integrator not exempt.

Eventually Congress will have to decide whether an industrial firm that has a farming operation can horn in on concessions granted farmers as small business units. Unless a legal distinction is made, the forecast made by Breimyer and Torgerson will be borne out: the concessions will be terminated.

Getting Cooperative Hands Slapped

In the last decade the most spirited cooperatives have been those in milk. Associated Milk Producers, Incorporated, won the most headline credit for its aggressions, whether deserved or not. It came under Department of Justice indictment. Meanwhile, the Federal Trade Commission got into the act, raising pointed questions particularly about marketing orders.

To some extent the unfriendly climate of the mid-1970s reflected persistent inflation in prices of farm products and food. Events then are traceable also to the deficiency of present law in spelling out what kinds of actions by farm groups are acceptable. Not only the Capper-Volstead Act is unclear. The Agricultural Marketing Agreement Act of 1937, the Agricultural Marketing and Bargaining Act of 1969, and other laws fail to delineate what practices come within antitrust immunity and what do not. Court decisions are a costly and at times acrimonious way of arriving at policy. Short of clarifying action by the Congress, the Court-test route is the only one available.

Nonetheless, the message and its warning are readily heard. Farmers' groups may continue to receive concessions but they will not extend to immunity from all regulation. The larger and more effective farmers' organizations become, the more they too will be subject to tests of performance in the public interest. That catechism is one of the non-blessings of gaining size and influence.

PROSPECTS

Farmers' ingrained resistance to collective action, the several false starts mixed in with unquestioned successes, and a general malaise about the whole subject during the boom times of the early 1970s—all these augur only continued uncertainty for at least the near future.

Not mentioned above are the issues of internal democracy in group action. One reason farmers are slow to commit their decision-making role to even their own organizations is that they believe their voices to be lost in the crowd. They allege that their cooperatives and other organizations are not truly democratic, despite their democratic trappings.

Yet one word remains to be said. If the marketing system is big and powerful in the commodity trading world, it is equally so in the political world. Farm leaders discovered this fact of life to their surprise and dismay when they lobbied for enactment of the bargaining law referred to above. Food processors demonstrated enough power to turn the tables almost 180 degrees against what farmers had sought. For instruction drawn from this experience, Torgerson's account is enlightening (2).

U.S. agriculture is still far removed from achieving group consciousness, let alone engaging in group action either to defend or to replace its philosophies and its institutions inherited from an earlier agrarian era. Instances of overaggressiveness by a farmers' group, such as a dairy cooperative, mask the impotence of most of agriculture. The ultimate irony may be the exploitation, not by farmers but by their agribusiness adversaries, of concessions an indulgent Congress has granted farmers.

NOTES

1. Harold F. Breimyer and Randall E. Torgerson, "Farmers' Cooperatives—By Whom and For Whom?" *Economic and Marketing Information for Missouri Agriculture,* Cooperative Extension Service (Columbia: Univ. of Missouri, April 1971).
2. Randall E. Torgerson, *Producer Power at the Bargaining Table* (Columbia: University of Missouri Press, 1970).

There is little evidence that we can predict accurately the future course of our world markets and therefore of our agriculture. Nevertheless . . . there are policy steps which we can take which will make the future more livable for all of us.

—V. J. RHODES

12 THE FOOD RESERVE ISSUE

A quirk about debate on farm policy is that the amount of noise made bears little relation to the gravity of an issue.

Some important matters such as vanishing of central markets scarcely bring a whimper of regret. Such minor ones as beef imports stir passions into flame.

Lawrence Simerl, longtime extension economist at the University of Illinois, has declared that the exposure given a policy issue is governed not by its economic significance but by its membership-attracting power. Beef imports are an example of what every membership secretary loves. They do not affect agriculture very much but they offer a surefire pitch to enlist members in a protest organization. Hence it becomes strategic to exaggerate and dramatize the price effect of imports.

Equally quixotic is factual accuracy in arguments. Some topics are discussed knowledgeably. Sound decisions usually follow. Others are treated as fantasy. Some pamphleteers could get high grades in a fiction-writing course.

The food reserve issue ranks among those that quickly stir interest and even antagonisms. It brings heat without much light. It gets more debate than factual analysis. In a sense the issue is important but it is not difficult to handle and not deserving of so much dissension.

Both the blessings of having food reserves and the dangers of not having them are easily overdrawn. Particularly is this true so long as the United States avoids any food-supply commitment to its customers—customers at home and export customers abroad.

If our nation should someday decide to establish goals for how well it feeds its own people and how considerately it responds to food needs worldwide, food reserves will truly deserve prominence. Reserve stocks are the only means by which unstable production can be converted to stable distribution. Such a noble dedication is not in prospect for the near future.

ANTAGONISTS

The debates of our time have little to do with any elevated goals for either food supply or the farm economy. At the mid-1970s they were mainly a matter of interest groups in opposition. Commercial grain producers opposed rebuilding reserves of grain. Livestock and poultry producers, exporters, and consumers were generally more favorable to reestablishing reserves. The grain people, reasoning that in 1973–75 we had no reserves and prices were high, concluded that avoiding reserves would help keep prices up. Feeders, exporters, and consumers saw reserves as a desirable stabilizer of supply and price and a protection against calamity.

Arguments the contenders offered pro and con were not so much mistaken as blown out of proportion. It is true that if the Commodity Credit Corporation had held grain into the inflation of the 1970s the price of grain would not have skyrocketed to the peaks it reached. A side question is whether such temporary bursts in price were good even for grain farmers. Nonetheless the strong demand of those years would have kept prices relatively high, reserves or no reserves.

In the same vein, availability of CCC stocks would have spared livestock and poultry people some of their 1973–74 tribulations and would have kept more of them in business. But the CCC could not have prevented a substantial rise in price of feed grains and soybean meal during those years.

MISREADING OF THE 1933–72 HISTORY

During most of the 40 years beginning in 1933 stocks of grain and cotton were held by farmers under price support loan, or by the CCC. Only briefly during that period were stocks depleted. Even after 1972 the program was not ended. It was only inoperative.

Much of the 1933–72 history has been misread.

Policy makers of the early 1930s did not set out to have a reserve program. The original object in commodity programs was to lend farmers money so that they could avoid having to sell their products on the depressed harvesttime market, which usually was the low for the year. By using CCC loans farmers could hold their crops for sale later.

As things worked out, sometimes markets failed to strengthen enough to allow the farmer to recover the loan price. Thereupon the

CCC found itself taking over grains and cotton under the "nonrecourse" terms of the loans. Unwittingly, the CCC got into the reserve business.

Rather quickly, the operation became redefined—legitimized, some would say—into a reserve storage plan. The Joseph account from Genesis was quoted, and the new concept was called "Ever-Normal Granary." (Agriculture Secretary Henry Agard Wallace had reportedly coined the term while an Iowa editor, but it was reintroduced only after the New Deal programs had been underway for some time. See *Century of Service*, U.S. Department of Agriculture, 1963.) Thereafter, commodities were to be accumulated in years when crops were large or demand weak, and released when opposite conditions prevailed.

Inasmuch as pressure was intense to keep price support loan rates well above market levels, in most years commodities were acquired by the CCC. More rarely were they released commercially. Stocks were drawn on freely during World War II, the Korean conflict, and the inflation of the early 1970s. They were released also during the payment-in-kind programs of the early 1960s. But otherwise they were mainly shipped abroad under Food for Peace.

Production outran demand at support prices so regularly during the 1933–72 period that the loan rate often became the market price. The net effect of the program therefore was to lift prices, on the average, above what they would have been without the program.

Even when stocks were largest, they did not and could not affect current market prices materially until those prices moved up close to the release-price level. Only occasionally did market prices strengthen that much. Contrary to opinion expressed in farm circles, seldom did CCC stocks act as a ceiling on prices. (Release of stocks under the payment-in-kind provisions of the early 1960s was a special case.)

Like the Russians, Americans engage in historical revisionism now and then. This has been happening regarding the history of our reserves. There is nothing mysterious about how grain reserves affect current prices. When stocks are large and growing, prices hug the support level. When stocks are being reduced by commercial sale, prices hug the release price level. When current production and demand are about in balance and stocks are stable, prices bob about between loan and release prices. That's all there is to it.

On the other hand, in a quirk that both supporters and opponents of reserves seem to overlook, the size of stocks affects prices indirectly through their bearing on the loan rate. If the price support-storage program works badly and stocks get too big, the political result is to keep loan rates relatively low. When stocks are small, it is safer to push the loan rates higher.

Big supplies in storage act to depress not market prices as such, as opponents allege so glibly, but the level of support prices that is politically feasible.

INDUSTRIAL DEMANDS ON AGRARIAN AGRICULTURE

Two basic facts will lay the groundwork for considering the place of food reserves. Neither is notably dramatic.

First, whenever and to whatever degree price support loans are used to underpin farmers' income, commodity storage is set in motion. This is the way it was during 1933–72, and this is the way it will be in at least the immediate future. Stocks may be in farmers' or CCC hands, but by their very nature price support operations involve at least the possibility of some year-to-year commodity storage.

Second, there is no cause for using scare language to advocate food reserves. Not having government reserves will not mean that U.S. consumers will be dangerously short of food in a bad crop year. We feed almost three-fifths of our grain to livestock and poultry and export another fourth. By slaughtering livestock, limiting exports, and shifting to a grain diet, we could survive any calamity. Bare survival is not at stake.

Having said that, we recognize that Americans of the 1970s do not want to settle for bare survival. Our economy is finely tuned, and we set high expectations for it.

Another way to put it is to sketch the contrast once again between agrarian and industrial thinking about agriculture. Our agriculture is part agrarian, part industrial. The casual, even callous, attitudes we have had toward reserves and dependability of the food supply fit with agrarian concepts. Nature supplies human needs variably and the appropriate response, in the agrarian tradition, is stoic acceptance or even fatalism. Furthermore, when harvests are small the "natural" response is for farmers to take care of their families' needs first, and to supply our cities next. Anything that remains can be shipped to far off lands.

In sharp contrast, everything that is industrial about our agriculture and its markets calls for finely tuned regularity and reliability. It demands a stability that conflicts with the notorious instability of the agrarian half of agriculture. Moreover, industrial agriculture is commercial. It puts each farmer under heavy financial commitment and makes him far more vulnerable to erratic prices than was the oldtime man-on-land agrarian. The farmer himself needs some stability.

Commercialization of much of our livestock and poultry offers a good example. When livestock were raised on family farms the size of herds was adjusted up and down on each farm in line with its harvests. Now that sizable operations are set up commercially and most of the feed is purchased, sharp fluctuations in feed prices can be adjusted to only with difficulty—sometimes only via bankruptcy proceedings for recapitalizing.

It is hardly necessary to add that food processing and retailing firms are geared to a steady supply of raw products. Erratic volumes add to cost. And even though U.S. consumers are never in danger of destitution, they clearly prefer a reliable supply of food at reasonably stable prices. During a flurry of food prices a few years ago they organized protest groups, became more active politically, and even staged a boycott.

Stabilization and the Export Market

Nowhere do issues in commodity stabilization come into sharper focus than in relation to export markets for farm products.

The United States is now a major food supplier to the world. It cannot be cavalier about its place in the world food system.

In down-to-earth honesty, the United States has treated its export markets with disdain. In the atmosphere of the mid-1970s it would be easy, and even correct, to recount with indignation how for years we begged, cajoled, and bribed (i.e., subsidized) foreign buyers to take our products, and then on three occasions in the 1970s preemptorially embargoed exports. Paradoxically, the embargoes probably were defensible in an ad hoc sense, and the greater guilt is that for decades we regarded foreign markets as a convenient depository for our surpluses without obligation to sustain them—and then did not sustain them.

More correctly stated, export markets have been subordinated to our domestic policy and seldom elevated to a respectable status of their own.

The big expansion in commercial exports of our farm products during the early 1970s coincidental with exhaustion of our surplus reserves, and our avowed wish to hold the export market, compels new attention to the meaning of stabilization. If export markets are to be kept, a reciprocal obligation is necessarily assumed, tacitly or openly. Japan dare not buy from us year after year unless we can deliver year after year. If we want the Japanese market we must be able to promise our capacity to supply it. It is the same with other regular buyers.

But the export picture does not end there. If in addition we want to take advantage of short-term, nonrepeatable demands, such as Russia's extraordinary buying following its droughts, we can do so only if we have salable supplies on hand. As James Rhodes puts it, "A major exporter cannot operate from bare shelves" (1).

The logical conclusion overwhelms: to be a major food exporter requires elevating foreign trade to status of its own. That in turn mandates a commodity reserve policy. A Breimyer proposal has been that a buffer stock should be set up for guaranteeing export deliveries. It could be separate from domestic reserve programs.

Even at this point the topic is not ended. Our export buyers could well accept some obligation toward regularity and dependability in their buying. If the United States should be willing to promise deliverability, her buyers ought to promise some certainty of acceptance. It would be a quid pro quo.

It is almost a parlor game for U.S. farm leaders to deplore the farm policies of the European Common Market on grounds that they reduce Europe's buying from us. A more valid complaint is that the Market treats us as residual suppliers of their needs. Although this is a perhaps justified counterpart of our treating Europe (and other export buyers) as residual outlets, the consequence is to keep foreign trade unstable, volatile.

According to this line of argument, the trade "understandings" our government has reached with Russia, Japan, and a scattered few other buyers of our grain classify as fitting the industrial part of agriculture. They are a radical but timely departure from agrarianism.

World Food Issues

When the United States had an embarrassing surplus of farm products it was conspicuously charitable with it. Food for Peace shipments to poor peoples of the world were life sustaining. According to an Iowa State University study, and contrary to much armchair opinionating, they did not of themselves restrain indigenous food production very much. On balance they served many human needs.

In the 1970s, when the world food situation turned into crisis, U.S. surpluses were gone. Concessionary shipments were cut back sharply.

The moral to be drawn is that our nation has been as cavalier about its concessionary food exports as about commercial ones.

So long as we stay with that attitude there is no need to fret about food reserves in relation to world food needs. Americans have sung paeans of self-praise about the trickle of food they have sent abroad in relief of hunger. But the 1½ million tons of grain shipped yearly as grants (gifts) and 3–5 million as concessionary sales are tiny relative to commercial exports of nearly 100 million tons. (Data are for the mid-1970s.) At this volume, talk about needing a reserve for food aid is pointless.

A case can be made on humanitarian as well as political grounds that our nation ought to commit itself more positively to assume a world food role. No challenge will be offered here. Yet again the soul torment could be overdramatized. Even at their peak, Food for Peace shipments were an insignificant portion of our total food supply. Having reserve stocks of grain would doubtless make concessionary exporting somewhat easier. But unless and until we make a lot bigger world food commitments than we have to date, the reserve issue is almost irrelevant. What matters most is simply whether we as a people (or someone) is willing to pay the cost. Dollars (or marks, francs, pounds, or yen) are the limiting factor, not the availability of grain.

Civil Defense Reserve

It's grim even to think about it, but most debates about food reserves omit one starkly sobering consideration. It is that we might need reserves sometime by virtue of military conflict abroad or civil disturbance at home. Heaven's blessings may shine on the United States of America but they grant no immunity from destruction wrought by selfish humanity. Our national efforts at civil preparedness have almost ended. Yet hazards are highlighted for us when we realize that most of our citizens live in cities that depend on a steady flow of food, and further that our food processing industries are highly vulnerable to casualty of power supply or transport.

DOING WHAT COMES NATURALLY—IF WE DON'T TRY FOR MUCH

This essay began with a warning against getting too excited about unexciting issues. Perhaps the paragraph above reexcites, although even a civil defense food reserve could be managed readily if we tried.

The big reason for staying in low key about food storage programs is that so long as our food concerns are muted the programs almost take care of themselves. They self-destroy and they self-create. During a price boom such as 1973–74 reserve stocks are certain to deplete and no new ones of substantial size can be accumulated. If at other times commodity supplies get too big and their prices toboggan downward, ideological protests quickly self-silence, effective price supports self-reestablish, and reserve stocks self-reappear.

All this holds true if we set no different standards of performance in the future than in the past. But if instead we aspire to a more stable food supply and trade, policy decisions will change. If we gear our agricultural policy to fit an industrial nation that wants to treat its citizens well and to be a strong force in both commercial export trade and world food aid, a commodity stabilization program will be essential. It will invariably contain some kind of reserve storage activity.

Program Design

Equally important as deciding whether to have reserves is to choose wisely how they are handled. Capsule suggestions follow:

1. The terms of a program should be firm and announced annually in advance of the planting and marketing season. These include the terms for release of stocks.

2. The spread between support and release prices should be wide enough to allow some room for market fluctuation. The 15 percent spread contained in the 1970 and 1973 laws was too narrow.

3. Both support and release prices should be kept flexible and adjusted so that the size of reserves moves up and down within limits set

for it. If stocks seem likely to grow too large, the two prices would have to be lowered. If bins empty too often, the prices would go up.

The quantity of stocks held will of course fluctuate. They are supposed to. The term "ever-normal granary" is a misnomer. More accurate would be "ever abnormal granary" for the object is to normalize not the size of stocks but current utilization.

4. It follows from (3) that price supports must be set with an eye on how stocks will be affected and not solely according to an income goal for farmers. Least of all can they be set high enough to cover all costs of farm production including land cost.

5. The general public will bear the cost of a storage program. No credence should be given the idea that farmers will themselves carry an adequate reserve of grains and cotton, at their own expense. They can afford to do so only when the market is on a sustained uptrend. When the outlook is for declining prices, farmers will not hold big quantities of reserves and ought not be expected to.

6. It does not matter who holds the commodities, provided integrity be assured. But both financing and control, including control over release, must come from government.

Other sources of ideas on how to set up a reserves program are found in Rhodes (1) and Robinson (2).

NOTES

1. V. James Rhodes, "Agricultural Production, Price, and Income Policy Within a National Economic Policy," *In Search of a U.S. Food Policy,* Agricultural Experiment Station Special Report 183 (Columbia: Univ. of Missouri, 1976), p. 23.
2. K. L. Robinson, "Unstable Farm Prices: Economic Consequences and Policy Options," *Am. J. Agr. Econ.* 57 (1975): 769–77.

Never will man penetrate deeper into error than when he is continuing on the road which has led him to success.

—F. A. VON HAYEK

13 DENOUEMENT

These essays were writtten during a period of relative calm. Mid-1976 to early 1977 was a time that could be called an interlude of euphoria. Although a few farmers regretted holding their grain too long and blamed "government" for their speculative losses, farm incomes were holding up surprisingly well. Not a few farm leaders concluded that God was in the marketplace again, and government could therefore keep out. Only for wheat did a new price distress seem imminent.

The principal topic of interest in farm circles was how to minimize income and estate taxes.

Prices of food had at least eased in their climb to an inflationary summit. The Secretary of Agriculture again promised big crops and little further increase in food prices.

Amateurs could feel secure. Veterans would remind how false any such feeling is.

AN EVER-CHANGING SCENE

More certain in agriculture than death and taxes is inconstancy. The economic position of farmers can change fast and radically. Sympathetic consequences are felt throughout the food system, and in the rural community as well.

The point to be drawn for our purpose is not the stabilization ingredient in farm policy. That was touched on several times in previous chapters. Rather to be emphasized is how rapidly the climate for making policy can flip from hot to cold, from interventionism to inaction, from considerate concern to cold indifference.

John Schnittker has written that "circumstances dictate policy" (1). The observation is shrewd.

Most kaleidoscopic of all may be farmers' attitudes. It has been suggested that when a farmer comes into a thousand dollars he takes on the philosophic complexion of a millionaire. Let him lose a thousand and he reverts to acting like a Populist radical.

Is it good to form farm policy on such a situation-of-the-moment basis? The question is scarcely different from the debate about whether it is better to be pragmatic or ideological. The record of policymaking has been relatively pragmatic. Yet we hear entreaties to draw up, once and for all, a truly comprehensive national farm and food policy. Probably a lasting overall policy is too much to hope for. Yet the vote is for a solid thrust in the direction. Much can be said in favor of doing so. Only by continuing commitment can some of the longer range problems, such as land use, be dealt with and goals pursued.

PERSONAL VERSUS NATIONAL FOCUS

In another sense, the question is not the comprehensiveness or (hoped for) permanence of a policy, but its focus. Does it aim at the welfare of individuals, or is it concerned only with big national magnitudes?

On this choice a middle ground, or a mixture of both, may be best.

In these essays partiality has been shown toward the operating farmer, the cultivator of land and caretaker of animals. This puts the author deep in the agrarian tradition. According to that tradition land becomes productive only upon applying labor and management plus associated risk—managerial risk, not investment risk. Land itself is only mineral ash, cosmic stuff, inert and worthless. The human being makes it produce.

The bias in favor of the working farmer carries a matching favoritism among kinds of return. In these lines return to the farmer's labor and management has been regarded more highly than unearned rentier income and capital gain.

But if we personalize concern for the individual farmer, out of respect for democratic values we must do likewise for other groups affected by farm policy. We cannot think in terms only of how much food is produced and what average rates of consumption are. We must consider also how well poor people eat. Gluttons boost the average!

Farmers find it difficult to empathize with persons they displace as they enlarge their own operations. But those persons count too.

The ultimate in considerateness is that for the welfare of babies to be born into future generations.

Perhaps personalizing of economic policy is a luxury. Surely the style in the mid-1970s runs in the other direction. We are drifting back to considering gross magnitudes and broad trends.

Authors of a Canadian study remarked on the same dual and vacillating focus to policy. Noting that "governments in Canada have always given agriculture . . . special status," they point out that "the orientation of that status was towards aiding and protecting the farmer."

Furthermore, "food was a subordinate concern to the producer's welfare." But if the public of Canada (or of the United States) henceforth feels insecure about its food supply, producers' interests would be "subordinated to national food objectives." This would be a "substantial policy shift indeed" (2).

NATIONAL GOALS FOR AGRICULTURAL POLICY

If we now turn to national goals for agricultural policy we say once more that policymaking cannot be parochial. In the language of my statement presented to a committee of the U.S. Senate,

In the final analysis, policy for agriculture must fit with the more elevated long-run goals set for the Nation as a whole. They are economic goals but they are social and political goals too.

Whatever challenges are seen for our Nation, agriculture must give its aid toward meeting them and agricultural policy must be drawn up accordingly. If those challenges are to arrest inflation, or to provide food for other nations, or to conserve land resources, or to husband depletable resources, agricultural policy is affected. Likewise if our goals include protecting the rural community, or resisting further concentration of economic power, or keeping pure water plentiful and the air clean. In all these, implications for agricultural policy are unavoidable (3).

The Mystical Future

All else aside, production of food and other fruit of the soil essential to human existence has an other-worldly quality, ephemeral, almost spiritual. This is the more so insofar as we have a sense of human destiny. Do we see ourselves as not only precursing but providing for future generations? In the turgid but impressive prose of Heilbroner, do we want the "unbearable anguish" we will feel if we "imagine ourselves as the executioners of mankind?" Or do we possess a "survivalist ethic" and share at least something of "the furious power of the biogenetic force we see expressed in every living organism?" (4)

To engage in farming while sensing a cosmic destiny for humanity moves us to protect our farming resources. It supports conservation practices and the preservation of farmland for farming. Farmland must be preserved if our descendants are to live.

Goals for agriculture can take on other dimensions according to time and place. As depletable minerals near exhaustion, will agriculture share in economizing and reclaiming (recycling)? Or will it enjoy such a priority that it can be irresponsible?

Agriculture in an industrial age has minimized its direct use of labor as it freed workers for urban industry. If urban employment decreases, it might be important to provide more opportunity once again for work in farming.

Another goal for agriculture is to deal kindly with its own. This militates against sharp divisions of class and income within agriculture. The goal comes hard; farmers are as quick as anyone to rationalize wealth-getting for the fortunate alongside poverty for the disadvantaged. Income distribution within agriculture is as uneven—as "skewed"—as in any part of the economy. Insofar as farm programs of the future involve paying out Treasury dollars, the program-voting, tax-paying public will likely be circumspect as to who gets how much.

AN AGRARIAN AND (PARTIALLY) INDUSTRIAL AGRICULTURE

A theme that recurs in these essays is the distinction between the agrarian and industrial parts of today's agriculture. It explains many contrasts and conflicts. Farm people are steeped in agrarianism. So, perhaps, are city people in their thinking about farming.

A tenet of agrarianism is a farmer's independence. As agriculture becomes more industrialized that independence becomes a casualty. The modern farmer is at the mercy of the rest of the economy. An embargo on Arabian oil could stop tractors. Not long ago a Missouri freeze cut off electric power and left cows unmilked. The industrial part of agriculture gives rise to a critical interdependence that was absent in ancient agrarianism.

This alone explains why farm policy is no longer the farmer's private prerogative.

It also explains farmers' frustrations. Agrarian farmers wrestled with soil and climate and they learned to do it rather well. Industrial farmers wrestle with each other, with their supply and product markets, and with tax collectors. Rhodes expresses these ideas in other language: Farming was once, he says, "a game of people against nature" but "our postindustrial economy is a game of people against people." Further, "farmers are comfortable" with the old game but "they generally prefer to pretend that they don't engage in games against people. . . . The dislike of farmers and their leaders for this new power game is exceeded only by their lack of skill in playing it" (5).

POLICY FOR WHAT KIND OF FARMING?

Farm policy is unique not only to its time and place but to its kind of farming. "Kind" in this sense means its structural type.

Policymaking in a democracy is packed with anomaly and contradiction—with paradox. Agricultural policy in the United States has long been designed for the needs, if not dedicated to the preservation, of a dispersed proprietary agriculture—the family farm. In the Breimyer language, it has been aimed at helping small agriculture survive in a big world (6).

Not just income policy but research and education and cooperative law and rural facilities funds (electrification and a dozen others) came into being as aids to the kind of agriculture that has prevailed in most of our nation since its birth. It is the kind where the farmer performs multiple roles including risk-bearing and gets composite returns. It is the family farm.

Some policy has truly supported the family farm. Some other laws were intended to do so but have been ambiguously successful. This judgment applies to theAgricultural Adjustment Act of 1938 and its successors, including laws of the 1970s. Meanwhile various other economic policies, notably tax shelters, are clearly destructive of the family farm.

The family farm is essentially an institution of agrarian agriculture. If agriculture of today had severed agrarian ties, structural issues of "who will control?" would disappear. It manifestly has not done so. It will not do so until food nutrients are fabricated in laboratories. Agriculture is now suspended between agrarian forces on the one hand and industrial ones on the other. And if the latter have grown more powerful in our century, the changed availability of industrial materials may lately be reversing the tide. If so, structural issues loom more prominently, not less.

The family farm is an institution not only of agriculture but of the rural community. Its fate has a meaning that transcends either the status of farmers or the state of the food supply.

More than that, the family farm has a symbolic significance to the entire community, urban as well as rural, as Griswold pointed out a generation ago (see Chapter 9).

THE "HOW" OF POLICYMAKING
It should be clear by now that farmers do not enjoy autonomy over the making of agricultural policy. During the 1973–75 period of buoyant prices some farmers thought they did—or should. Not a chance! As extension economists put it, using words reminiscent of the comedian Jimmy Durante, "Today everybody is getting into the act" (7).

Policymaking in a democracy is not very systematic. As much as anything it is a means of mutual accommodation. It requires a basic consensus of purpose but in other respects it is more a matter of developing workable compromises than of forming clear-cut policy directives.

The agrarian tradition that is still so strong impedes the compromise process. At the same time—an instance of paradox—some trends toward industrialization of agriculture have not helped either. This is especially true of greater specialization, which splits agriculture along commodity lines. Each commodity group wants to pursue its own interests. The coalition of farm organizations that has operated spasmodically in the 1970s is a heroic and sometimes effective effort to arrive at common policy ground.

To some extent nonfarm groups have a louder voice now because farmers themselves are so divided.

These comments bring us back to the idea of farmers' group consciousness. Farmers' difficulty in thinking in group terms is their worst handicap in addressing issues in policy. It is a mattter of thought habits, of inability to comprehend policies in terms of their generalized effect. Agrarian-rooted farmers are prone to individualize everything. In so doing—another paradox—they can misread even their own interests.

On the other hand, group consciousness does not mean that the solution requires group action. It may not. Thought habits and policy directions are two different subjects. They should not be confused.

BIOLOGICAL MAN AND SOCIAL ORGANIZATION

We end where we began, with biological man and social organization. Human beings, themselves biological but endowed with the gift of cognition, manage both the biological and the mineral world and do so by employing their capacity for social organization. So has it ever been. So will it ever be. The questions are eternal. The answers are temporal. Agricultural policy is made for its time and place; and it is made also for the kind of social as well as economic organization that is sought in the interests of farmers and of the rural community. But also in the largest sense it must be consonant with the ideals the nation itself declares for all its citizens.

NOTES

1. John A. Schnittker, "Alternative Food and Agriculture Policies for the United States," *Michigan Farm Economics,* Department of Agricultural Economics Paper No. 400, Cooperative Extension Service, (East Lansing: Michigan State University, May 1976), p. 1.
2. Food Prices Review Board, *Final Report of the Food Prices Review Board* (Ottawa, Canada: February 1976), p. 45.
3. Harold F. Breimyer, "Agriculture and the Economy," *Farm and Food Policy, 1977,* Committee on Agriculture and Forestry, U.S. Senate, 94th Cong., 2nd Sess. September 15, 1976, p. 40.
4. Robert L. Heilbroner, "What Has Posterity Ever Done for Me?" *New York Times Magazine* (January 19, 1975), p. 15.
5. V. James Rhodes, "Agricultural Production, Price, and Income Policy Within a National Economic Policy," *In Search of a U.S. Food Policy,* Agricultural Experiment Station Special Report 183 (Columbia: University of Missouri, 1976), p. 21.
6. Harold F. Breimyer, "The Inevitable Joining of Farm and Food Policy," J. S. McLean Memorial Lecture, University of Guelph, Ontario. Department of Agricultural Economics Paper No. 1975–10 (Columbia: University of Missouri).
7. Barry L. Flinchbaugh and Carole B. Yoho, "Politics and Food Policy," *Your Food: A Food Policy Basebook,* National Public Policy Education Committee Publication Number 5, Cooperative Extension Service (Columbus: Ohio State University, November 1975), p. 61.

A society organized solely on the principle of equality of opportunity is not acceptable, and one organized solely around the principle of equality of results would not be operational.
—Paul W. McCracken

I IN SEARCH OF THE GOOD SOCIETY

All human beings live in an ambiguous relation to the persons about them.

Each person wants very much to satisfy his own wants, to pursue his own affairs, to control his own destiny. We are all egocentric.

But we cannot do this in isolation. Scarcely a human need can be met without some form of social interaction. Humans are social creatures whether they wish to be or not.

These paired paradoxical axioms bring various ideas to mind. How much vain boasting is heard! The notion of the "self-made man or woman," and denial of social responsibility because "I earned what I have," are only, in the words of St. Paul, "sounding brass."

Another version is extreme patriotism, exalting one's own nation above all others. This could be the greater transgression, or the more dangerous.

Far sounder is an admission that all persons, irrespective of their skin-deep pride, must be concerned for their reciprocal relationships with society about them.

THE TEMPER OF OUR TIME

How well have we in the United States solved the riddle of relationship between each person and society? For years we sincerely believed that we had learned the lesson of democracy and could teach the world.

First published in *Economic and Marketing Information for Missouri Agriculture*. Univ. of Missouri-Columbia, May 1974. Slightly revised.

Signs are that we no longer feel so certain of it. Dr. Paul Mc-Cracken, quoted above, Chairman of the Council of Economic Advisers 1969–71, puts it that "the nation has witnessed an erosion of the underpinning consensus about our socio-economic system." Said more simply, we are in serious trouble and know it.

Whenever people are jarred badly enough they turn from superficial matters and reask the ageless questions. These are the same questions as were posed by the thinkers of ancient Egypt and Judea, and Greece and Rome; by the medieval churchmen; and by the great minds of the Enlightenment.

How indeed do we establish the good society?

A LIBERAL ECONOMY IN AN OPEN SOCIETY

Dr. McCracken summarizes the American dream in these words: "Ours was the concept of a liberal economy . . . characterized by free and open markets through which consumers expressed their preferences, and through which as producers we chose where and how to make our own contribution to the productive stream." He adds, "the energizing concept was that all should have equal opportunity and that material rewards should depend on accomplishment rather than the happenstance of hereditary privilege or race or political pull and influence." He explains further that this "was the Protestant Ethic in operation" and that the system was regarded as not only productive but "just and moral"(1).

Daniel Bell, a Harvard sociologist, declares that in this philosophy "the individual—and not the family, the community, or the state—is the basic unit of society, and . . . the purpose of societal arrangements is to allow the individual the freedom to fulfill his own purposes" (2).

These are high-sounding phrases. Why then do we have such seemingly unsolvable economic problems as inflation, a widening income gap between rich and poor, ever more divisiveness among social classes, crime high and low, and more political scandals than in a century?

There is no lack of explanations. Everyone has his favorite. Blame is often laid to a political or economic group (the devil syndrome), a kind of law, or a way of living. Such simple castigations won't do. Roots are deep, numerous, and complex.

But first, is "equality of opportunity" itself a satisfactory principle? The words are so appealing, but how do they translate into equality of opportunity for unequal people? This seems a brutal contradiction. "Equality" of opportunity will not care for the needs of the aged, the young, the handicapped.

Further, even for able middle-aged males, what does the principle mean if opportunity itself is limited? Does equal access to a restricted opportunity imply that the winner takes all? What happens to the loser?

Dr. McCracken does not ponder philosophy but strikes at our social failure to provide anything close to equal opportunity. Differences in "material emoluments of life" may reflect not effort so much as "random elements." This discouraging judgment applies particularly to children, he says, as he contrasts the "luck of the draw" that puts some children in "homes favoring achievement" and others "in a situation where their mothers could not even be sure about the identity of the fathers."

Nor is public education now trusted as the great equalizer. Dr. McCracken cites the 1966 Coleman report showing that schooling has much less bearing on individuals' achievement than is popularly believed.

In his scholarly language, Dr. McCracken admits to a suspicion that our "meritocracy" is "less distinguishable from a system of hereditary privilege than had been supposed."

The Social Mucilage

Dr. McCracken's words about hereditary privilege remind that liberal principles of social organization have been rare in the world's history. By far the most common means to bring individual conduct into social conformity has been coercion. Whether applied by monarchial or military rule, it has usually been accompanied by a caste or status-oriented society. Therein was the lot of each person largely prefixed.

About five centuries ago the Age of Reason in western Europe brought a new faith in the individual's ability to see his social obligation and govern his conduct accordingly. Rousseau said he would enter into "social contract." The founding father of economics, Adam Smith, went even further: under the proper economic organization the individual could pursue his selfish interests without fear of offending society.

This was the "concept of a liberal economy" to which Dr. McCracken referred. It was Western man's big opportunity.

Western man has botched it.

In some respects circumstances turned against him. Part of the motivation for our era was the chance to invade new continents for their lands, timber, minerals—and living room. Those continents are now packed with people, the land occupied and much of the resources exploited.

It is relatively easy to espouse liberal principles in a rural, agrarian setting. Urban industrial society requires more complex social organization.

But the fatal error arises not so much in circumstances as in people themselves and the institutions they create. Liberal ideas do not perpetuate themselves unattended. They must be defended. Laisser faire, the old French doctrine of letting all things go, is false doctrine.

Limitation on Power

Basic to classical liberalism is limitation on power. Everyone can safely pursue his self interest provided no one has power over another. And if opportunity is to be kept open for all, no one shall be allowed to foreclose it.

This prerequisite has been violated blatantly. Evidence is overwhelming. Every new episode in economic affairs, as of the 1973–74 fuel crisis, reveals how much economic power is concentrated in relatively few hands.

Political power likewise is no longer diffused. The federal government now holds some authority over almost every part of human existence.

The grand irony is that we as a nation have moved step by halting step into giant organizational structure while still professing all the ideology of a decentralized, equal-opportunity, "free-enterprise" system. Under the intellectual façade of a bygone day we harness ourselves into a new superstructure more powerful, and more ominous, than the medieval mercantilism from which the events of five centuries ago released us.

Truly, what we profess is in sharp contrast with what exists.

It would be better to be honest about the kind of economic and political system we have got ourselves into. We could then deal with it better.

A Syndicalistic Structure

Political and economic power is not confined to big business and big government. We are witnessing still another trend, one toward a huge network of affiliations. Indeed, insofar as the interests of the individual are still protected, his advocate and defender is likely to be the group of which he is a part.

This trend to affiliate is sometimes called syndicalism. The term applies to industrial unions, to business organizations with their lobbyists, to professional bodies such as the American Medical Association, to farmers' cooperatives and bargaining associations. We have a labyrinth of such organizations. They are a mark of our time.

Such organizations can in principle defend the interests of their members. But in another sense, the burden of concern for the opportunity of the individual is only shifted from society as a whole to the internal government of the organization. What assurance is there that a trade association, a labor union, or a farmer cooperative protects the interests of its members with equity and honesty?

The basic questions asked at the beginning of this article about the human being and society can be applied trenchantly to his organizations.

Moral Code as Foundation

Human society does not begin with institutions. It begins with the values and beliefs and moral qualities of individual persons. These in turn are a social product. Each generation ought to be circumspect as to the moral code it inherits, adapts, and passes on.

Dr. McCracken remarks on the "atrophy of religion, which has robbed our secular philosophy of its moral and spiritual foundation." Irving Kristol reminds that "social critics have been warning us that bourgeois society has been living off the accumulated moral capital of traditional religion and traditional moral philosophy." He adds that once this capital is depleted, that society will crumble (3).

We inherited a strict moral code, one with a religious base containing admonitions to personal discipline, charity, and nonmaterial values. Our choice has been to replace it with scientifically based secularism. Any vestige of medieval asceticism has given way to a materialism and sensuality comparable to that of debauched monarchs in earlier times.

Contributing to the change in our value system is the commercialization of social communication. No longer is the accumulated wisdom of a people put in the hands of its wiser men, its judges, scholars, teachers, and religious leaders. Instead, we huckster it. Not even the public schools any longer teach moral values (though teachers bootleg some). And in a misguided sense of liberalism we refuse to restrain the most pernicious mass communication other than outright personal libel, despite the fact that the survivability of a society rests on communicating its value system.

Equality of Results

Dr. McCracken says that we have found the principle of equality of opportunity so wanting or so unapplied that we have turned to equality of results as a replacement. He regrets the change yet admits that we probably cannot avoid it.

In a word, we set goals for various sectors of the economy and use the power of government to attain them. And, in line with the idea of our syndicalized grouping, he says we set the goals by group or category. We provide minimum income for our aged, minimum food for our poor; we set race quotas in hiring; we even consider assuring low I.Q. students access to college education.

As we turn to equality of results, we compromise the pricing system. We make it necessary to adopt some kind of income maintenance policy. We put ever more emphasis on the political process by which we define "equality" of results, and seek to attain it.

But Dr. McCracken adds that we will not go all the way. We will compromise equality of opportunity and of results. Hence his summary statement quoted at the heading of this essay.

Meaning to Agriculture

The meaning to agriculture is almost self-revealing. To some degree the farming community holds the more traditional values. But it also contains sharp economic and social cleavages within it. And although agriculture as a whole has accepted federal help conferred under the "equality of results" principle, it has not solved problems of internal equality among its own members.

Furthermore, in its pioneer era agriculture could readily live up to its principle of equal opportunity. Not so now. The door is being closed ever tighter against new entrants other than those who already possess considerable means.

Disturbing Portents

Any summary is highly personal. The author is apprehensive. In his judgment, while pursuing private gain and material values, and depending on rationality instead of religion to induce social responsibility, we have built the most complex and critically interdependent economy ever seen on this planet.

Each organized group, whether business, professional, or labor, has the capacity to disrupt the delicately poised mechanism. This is just as true of a firm that shuts down because profits are too small as of "radical" action. And the opportunities for individuals to violate social responsibility are legion.

Our kind of economy *must* have disciplined order. If it is not attained through the kind of liberal democratic processes that Dr. Mc-Cracken describes as our heritage, it will be imposed by authoritarian measures. Such a change has been made in Brazil, Chile, and several other formerly democratic nations. Almost always, the privileged property-holding class joins with military forces to impose the discipline. Suppression of the press and restriction on the flow of ideas are among the invariable consequences.

If that should be our destiny too, those who usurp power are not alone to be blamed. Not least among culprits will be the body of citizens who thought "search of the good society" meant pursuit of private indulgence without social discipline.

As concluding admonitions, let us look to our capacity to build a moral base for a good society; and insofar as we must seek equality of results instead of relying soley on equality of opportunity, let us be honest about it, stop pretending, and go to work on it. That means seeking out ways to get approximate equality of results; it means, too, cleaning up our capacity to govern ourselves democratically.

NOTES
1. Paul W. McCracken, "The New Equality," *Michigan Business Review* (University of Michigan, March 1974).
2. Daniel Bell, "On Meritocracy and Equality," *The Public Interest* (Fall 1973), p. 40.
3. Irving Kristol, "Capitalism, Socialism, and Nihilism," *The Public Interest* (Spring 1973), p. 12.

A general equality of condition is the true basis, most certainly, of democracy.

*—*DANIEL WEBSTER

II AGRARIANISM AND THE AMERICAN HERITAGE

Americans tried hard to observe their bicentennial pridefully. They staged the usual celebrations, performed proper rituals, self-declared that almost everything was all right.

They were less than fully successful.

It is not that new crises arose in 1976. The economy had improved. The riotous 1960s had been left behind. Watergate was past and Vietnam only a memory.

It was easy to cite genuine achievements in our national history. Truly, "much is right" with America.

Yet we had doubts even as we celebrated. Disappointments are easily named. They are as intimate as decline of the family and as global as our nation's lessened prestige internationally.

What is difficult is to agree on root causes. Our agrarian tradition may provide a focus for addressing that question.

The new United States was agrarian during its first century. It became steeped in agrarian values and accustomed to agrarian habits of thought. It is now urban and industrial, a different milieu. Some of the agrarian tradition has been retained. Much, however, has been lost. Are we the worse off therefor?

DIFFERENCE OF OPINION

Before proagrarians shout their "aye" let us remember that rural culture has always had a mixed press. On the one hand, ancients and moderns

First published in *Economic and Marketing Information for Missouri Agriculture,* University of Missouri-Columbia, July 1976. Slightly revised and updated.

alike have vied in tribute. Pliny the Elder wrote that "the agricultural population produces the bravest men, the most valiant soldiers, and a class of citizens the least given of all to evil design." Bernard Baruch declared, "The farm gives the nation men as well as food. Cities derive their vitality and are forever renewed from the country." The great seal of USDA inscribes, "Agriculture is the foundation of manufacture and commerce." Secretaries of Agriculture have competed in accolades. Henry A. Wallace: "Good farming; clear thinking; right living"; and Ezra Taft Benson: "The rural population is America's safeguard against foreign 'isms' and crackpot programs."

Other famous people have glorified the city and scorned everything rural. The Greek Euripides put it, "The first requisite to happiness is that a man may be born in a famous city." Henry David Thoreau updated in words that "it makes but little difference whether you are committed to a farm or a county jail." Forty years ago Joseph Davis, later an advisor to President Eisenhower, called proagrarian ideas "agricultural fundamentalism." He challenged its soundness, "not because there is no truth in it, but because it contains so much of error as to lead the world astray" (1).

CONFUSION IN MEANING

Some of the difference in opinion comes from differences in interpretation. In one sense agrarianism (or fundamentalism) means only that agriculture produces basic materials. More commonly, though, it applies to moral and social principles.

More confusing is the Jeffersonian version of agrarianism versus older concepts. Thomas Jefferson's agrarianism called for a nation of small landholders. Jefferson, though himself a big planter, saw them as the bedrock of democracy. His concept was sharply different from older agrarian systems. Historically most agriculture had been organized as tribal or nomadic units or as estates. They often rested on human slavery. The medieval estate of Europe was transplanted to the New World as plantation and hacienda. Both gave way to the family farm, as Jefferson had advocated, as the basic U.S. system.

AGRARIANISM AND PERSONAL DISCIPLINE

Agrarianism gave us several of our ideas and precepts. Some trace to Jeffersonianism and others to the older tradition. Still others are more general. Perhaps the most general of all is the relation of agrarianism to personal discipline.

Agrarianism is rooted in the forces and resources of "nature." Nature is bountiful. She also is imperious in her demands upon human conduct. Her processes are biological: both plants and animals must be cared for. They are sequential: the seed must be planted, and the fruit harvested, each in its own season.

As though to clinch the lesson, failure to follow nature's dictates brings its penalties. A crop untended yields no harvest. A cow unfed gives no milk. Cause and effect are thereby dramatized, with a moral message.

Agrarianism is often credited with engendering not only personal discipline but the work ethic.

AGRARIANISM AND REGARD FOR RESOURCES

All humanity relies on nature's dispensation of sun, soil, and rain. The dependency has led to responses ranging from frustration to gratitude. It has given rise to some nonethical pantheistic religions. Even today the Russians, dissuaded from Jewish or Christian worship, venerate Mother Earth.

The U.S. agrarian response has been mixed. Our Judeo-Christian heritage is positive but irresolute. The Psalmist gloried in the hills but none of Moses' ten commandments called for protecting resources. (Three concerned relations of man to God, seven of man to man.) The eminent soil conservationist of a generation ago, W. C. Lowdermilk, proposed an "eleventh commandment." "If Moses had foreseen what suicidal agriculture would do to the land of the holy earth—might [he] not have been inspired to deliver another Commandment to establish man's relation to the earth?"

Historically, the practice has been to abandon land ("suicidally") rather than to conserve it. Even today, after expenditures of billions of federal dollars land in our country is not protected fully against leaching and erosion. Equally important, nothing is being done to keep fertile farmland from being lost eternally to commercial and industrial uses.

And the depletable resources? Agrarianism does not even hint at conserving them. Lowdermilk today might ask for a twelfth commandment: "Thou shalt dole out thy petroleum and recycle thy metals, lest there be deprivation from generation unto generation."

AGRARIANISM AND A MARKET SYSTEM

The crucial issue about the Jeffersonian brand of agrarianism as contrasted with the older one lay not in forming small independent farms but in arranging their external connections. Such old agrarian units as the estate were almost self-sufficient internally. Jobs were assigned by mandate and rewards were divided arbitrarily. Not so with the new farm, in which internal support was reduced to the single family—although some neighborly help was given within a community, and still is.

The solution was to apply the lessons about market exchange that had been learned from Europe. The new farms were to buy and sell. Markets were to distribute products and establish value. The venture was heroic. In it a system of market relationships replaces the internal mutual support that was a mark of the older agrarian units.

AGRARIANISM, A MARKET SYSTEM, AND DEMOCRACY
As noted above, Jefferson's U.S. agrarianism was a part of the new and risky venture into democracy. A market system that works well fits with democracy. It is worth noting, though, that democracy was not itself of agrarian origin. Agriculture can take credit for largely developing the market system, which it then gave to burgeoning new industry. But democracy evolved among restive urban people while agriculture was still mired in feudalism. What the new agrarianism in our new nation did was to link independent farms, markets, and democracy together.

The merits of a system of markets within a democracy are readily seen. Buying and selling in open exchange allows individual independence and provides reward equivalent to performance. The capstone is that reward is determined impersonally, by market forces, and not according to the whims of an overlord.

WEAK POINTS IN A MARKET SYSTEM
If a market system has so many merits, why is ours fading (see below)? Have agrarian institutions let us down?

Paradoxically, the market system's strength—its latitude for so much individual independence—can also be its weakness. Three flaws come to mind.

First is simply to misread the situation, to fail to appreciate how interdependent a market system is. In the ancient agrarian units mutual support was self-evident. It was imposed but it was visible. Every person did his job, even under duress, in expectation that others would do theirs. In market exchange the interdependence is less obvious.

Second is the mistake of failing to recognize what a market system will *not* do. It will not offset severe personal adversity and it will not provide social services such as dredging a river or stopping environmental pollution. In this respect markets can be trusted too much.

The third error is to pay too little attention to the conditions necessary for a system to work well. A market system will neither self-create nor self-police. It is a legal creation that starts from enforceable laws of contract. From its beginning in England it required legal protections such as those against practices called, in quaint Old English, regrating, forestalling, and engrossing. Like democracy itself the system rests on a reasonably equitable status for all parties. When any trader gains dominant power, a market system becomes an agent of subservience and exploitation, not of equity.

To put it differently, the individualism of a market system can lead to an obliviousness of the very interdependence that the system so adroitly brings about. The consequence can be failure to guard the system's integrity.

DECLINE OF AGRARIAN MARKETS
Philosophizing apart, the hard fact is that the agrarian market system is fading from the scene. Industry has almost abandoned open trading markets in favor of merchandising. Only such marts as the stock exchange retain the old features. In agriculture only a few commodities have vigorous open markets. A seventh of all agriculture is contractually integrated, and a tenth is in large corporate hands. Several food processing industries are highly concentrated. Important export markets are closely tied to political relations among nations.

Jeffersonian agrarianism would call for revitalization of markets. It would begin with aggressive antitrust. The trend is opposite, and agriculture's recourse in this century has been toward group action that reverts not to Jefferson's but to ancient agrarianism.

These trends leave the agricultural community restive. They also wash out agrarianism's lessons to the general community. James Rhodes puts it in a sociologist's terms that farming was once "a game of people against nature" and farmers were comfortable with it. Our present economy including parts of agriculture, pits "people against people." Farmers, though quick to recite the old axioms, are not so sure how to deal with the new situation. Nor, apparently, are nonfarmers.

THE AGRARIAN WORK ETHIC
In the agrarian work ethic work is esteemed of itself and rewards are to be proportionate to productivity. The work ethic is under stress in bureaucratic business and industry, where "meaninglessness" is often charged. It is vulnerable to inflation.

Even in agriculture, events of recent years have yielded more return via capital gain than from the work of planting crops and feeding animals. Tax rules bear heavily on net incomes. If successful speculation and legal sleight of hand pay off better than plowing the field and hoping for rain, how can the work ethic stay unchallenged?

AGRARIAN EGALITARIAN DEMOCRACY TODAY
Jefferson saw comparative equality of status as essential to democracy, as did Webster and other national leaders.

When land was cheap and readily available, it was possible to give everyone minimum status.

Land is no longer cheap. Agriculture is not yet dominated by a few giants but it has its own class structure. Wealth and income are as unevenly divided there as elsewhere in the economy. If trends are away from a reasonably egalitarian balance within agriculture, they are therefore also away from Jeffersonian agrarian democracy.

AGRARIANISM AND OPPORTUNITY

According to all surveys, rural people endorse the principle of equality of opportunity. This is now more an adage than a reality. Present land prices almost foreclose opportunity to persons of modest means. Some farm leaders have advocated federal programs to finance carefully screened new farmers. Others, however, go the other direction as they want to reduce inheritance taxation—a measure that would reduce opportunity for new farmers. The conflict in principles is apparently not perceived.

AGRARIANISM AND BIG BUREAUCRACY

It hardly need be added that in the American agrarian tradition large size is distrusted in either private or public institutions. Bureaucracy is openly resented. Here too, though, a contradiction appears, and it may have meaning to our time. We distrust and resent but we do not restore. Who would end Social Security and make each family responsible for its elderly? If farm markets should break sharply in the next year or two, would farmers refrain from calling for higher price supports or payments?

SUMMARY COMMENTS

Words of Lincoln quoted recently call Americans a people "destitute of faith but terrified of skepticism." If we are mired in uncertainty and contradictions and need some restored faith, it is fitting to ask whether the agrarian tradition, so prominent during much of our national life, still has something to contribute.

This review is intended to be basically positive, if only because the reviewer is himself immersed in the work ethic and other agrarian values.

From ancient agrarianism we have the heritage of individual responsibility and the work ethic. From the Jeffersonian tradition we get market democracy, a heroic effort to allow maximum individuality while still synchronizing all parts of our interdependent system.

Both are wonderful legacies.

Despite them we are in trouble. Evidence is everywhere. We are becoming more polarized, more internally divided. Distrust seeps through both private affairs and government. In our bicentennial election year a number of candidates disparaged the office they ran for. Intellectual cynicism gives rank and file citizens an excuse for shady or even outright illegal behavior. If continued the trends lead to chaos and then to authoritarian rule.

So we ask again, in view of our grand agrarian legacies, what is amiss? Although there is room for various explanations, this reviewer's is that in accepting Jeffersonian agrarianism we lost sight of ancient agrarianism's lesson of binding unity. Call our situation individualism run amok or put the blame on our excessively large, disjoined, depersonalized business and governmental institutions—see it as one will, the words of Walter Lippmann written in 1929 come piercingly to mind. Lippmann said that modern man "does not find any natural substitute for those accumulated convictions which . . . organized his soul, economized his effort, consoled him, and gave him dignity in his own eyes because he was part of some greater whole."

There must be a tie to bind lest we all, in biblical and Shakespearean language, be "undone."

The individual can find his best destiny only within a social structure the integrity of which he himself must help guarantee. This rule seems the best distillate of agrarianism, ancient *and* modern.

NOTES
1. Several quotations are taken from Calvin Beale in *Agricultural Science Review,* second quarter 1971.

INDEX